CAMBRIDGE TEXTS AND STUDIES IN THE HISTORY OF EDUCATION

General Editors

A.C.F.BEALES, A.V.JUDGES, J.P.C.ROACH

H. E. ARMSTRONG
AND THE TEACHING OF SCIENCE
1880–1930

IN THIS SERIES

H. E. ARMSTRONG

AND THE TEACHING OF SCIENCE
1880–1930

EDITED WITH AN INTRODUCTION BY

W. H. BROCK

LECTURER IN HISTORY OF SCIENCE
UNIVERSITY OF LEICESTER

CAMBRIDGE
AT THE UNIVERSITY PRESS
1973

Published by the Syndics of the Cambridge University Press
Bentley House, 200 Euston Road, London NW1 2DB
American Branch: 32 East 57th Street, New York, N.Y. 10022

Library of Congress Catalogue Card Number: 72–87179

ISBN 0 521 08679 5

Printed in Great Britain
by William Clowes & Sons, Limited
London, Beccles and Colchester

Contents

Note on the Selections

Almost all of Armstrong's large output of miscellaneous essays that are not primarily concerned with original scientific matters deal with education either directly or indirectly. Only twenty-five of these essays were reprinted in his *Teaching of Scientific Method*. I have used two criteria for selecting items from these educational essays. First, any items which played an essential historical role in the adoption of heuristic and laboratory methods in schools demanded attention. This group includes the 'inaugural' lecture of 1884, the British Association report and syllabus of 1889, and the Board of Education special report on heurism of 1898. To be sure, all these items were included in *Scientific Method*; and this has been out of print since 1925. In the present case the original printed versions have been followed. Secondly, I have wished to illustrate Armstrong in polemical and historical mood. Unfortunately, lack of space has limited selection from this genre to the semi-autobiographical essay on Huxley, Armstrong's contribution to Spencer's *Aims and Practice of Teaching*, 1897, a section from the Mosely report, and the meditative and disillusioned reflection on Sanderson of 1924. A chronological order has been followed after the Huxley Memorial Lecture of 1933.

Editorial deletions are indicated by the ellipsis, while additions to the texts are indicated by square brackets. Notes to the Introduction and to the selections, which are indicated by superscript numerals, are gathered at the end, and in both these, the place of publication is London unless otherwise indicated.

Acknowledgements

I should like to record my gratitude to the late Miss Nora Armstrong for her interest and the gift of Dr Eyre's biography of her father, which proved invaluable in the preparation of the Introduction. I am indebted to Messrs Macmillan (London and Basingstoke) the original publishers of *Scientific Method*, for their co-operation and goodwill. Mrs Jeanne Pingree, custodian of Armstrong's letters and offprints at Imperial College Archives, London, generously provided me with facilities and enthusiasm. Mrs Margaret Findlay kindly gave me secretarial assistance. My own interest in heurism was first aroused by Drs R. A. R. Tricker and C. A. Russell. Two former Leicester students, Mr K. Armitage and Mrs J. H. Harris, stimulated and maintained it during their studies for the Diploma in Philosophy and History of Education. My introduction has benefited from the advice of Professor A. V. Judges, who has shown great patience in dealing with a relative newcomer to the History of Education. I am grateful to all of them.

Leicester University
February 1972   W.H.B.

Abbreviations

A.P.S.S.M.	Association of Public School Science Masters
B.A.R.	*Reports of the British Association for the Advancement of Science*
Browne	C.E. Browne, *Henry Edward Armstrong*, priv. printed, Harrison & Sons, London, Hayes, and High Wycombe, 1954 (reprinted with a Memoir of Browne 1968)
C.	*The Central* (Journal of the Central Institution Old Students Association)
Cardiff	H.E. Armstrong, *The Extension of British Trade*, Cardiff Education Committee, Cardiff, 1915
D.N.B.	*Dictionary of National Biography*
D.S.A.	Department of Science and Art
E.T.	*Educational Times*
Eyre	J.V. Eyre, *Henry Edward Armstrong*, 1958
I.C.A.	Imperial College Archives, London
I.C.E.	*International Conference on Education Proceedings*, 4 vols., 1884 (in some series labelled vols. 13–16 of *International Health Exhibition Literature*)
J.S.C.I.	*Journal of the Society of Chemical Industry*
Kensington	H.E. Armstrong, *Pre-Kensington History of the Royal College of Science and the University Problem*, 1921
N.	*Nature*
R.C.C.	Royal College of Chemistry
R.I.C.	*Journal and Proceedings of the Royal Institute of Chemistry*
Ross	W. Ross, *Teacher's Manual of Method, or the General Principles of Teaching and Schoolkeeping*, 1848
Selleck	R.J.W. Selleck, *The New Education 1870–1914*, 1968

S.M.	H. E. Armstrong, *The Teaching of Scientific Method and Other Papers on Education* (all references are to the 1925 edition)
S.R.	*Special Reports on Educational Subjects*
S.S.R.	*School Science Review*
Thomson	J. J. Thomson *et al.*, *Natural Science in Education*, 1918

Thoughts hardly to be packed
Into a narrow act,
Fancies that broke through language and escaped;
All I could never be,
All men ignored in me,
This, I was worth to God, whose wheel the pitcher shaped.

Scored by Armstrong against his copy of
Browning's *Rabbi Ben Ezra*

Editor's Introduction

'Better late than never, it is said. A sudden breakdown in health forces me to realise that it must be now, if ever. The proverbial ill-wind helps me by dropping me upon the chalk at Eastbourne, in the house that Huxley built when he retired.' Unfortunately Armstrong did leave it too late, and he completed only a fragment of autobiography.[1] On the other hand, many of his essays and obituary notices of friends and colleagues have an autobiographical flavour, so that a composite picture of his career and the events which shaped it can be easily assembled.

Henry Edward Armstrong was born at Lewisham, Kent, on 6 May 1848, as the first of seven children of Richard Armstrong (1827–84), a London scrivener who had romantically eloped and married Mary Ann Biddle a year previously. After marriage his father had taken up a new trade as a French agent for grocery provisions, and this international business provided the growing Armstrong family good contacts with the City of London which were to be cultivated by Henry throughout his life. Richard Armstrong, a largely self-educated man, was an omnivorous reader and he encouraged this recreation in Henry – his favourite child. Many City friends were entertained at Lewisham, some of whom like Klassen, a Dutch merchant at the London Corn Exchange who was an active geologist, or the wheat-merchant Kekulé, the half-brother of the famous chemist, brought with them a repertoire of scientific gossip and comment. In the 1860s Lewisham, which is now part of Greater London, was still a country town divided in two by the unpolluted river Ravensbourne. Some of Armstrong's strongest memories were of out-of-doors pursuits as a child when his deep love of Nature was founded. Then, *Emile*-like he discovered the Cosmos, scrambling over clay and chalk, exploring chalk-pit pools, or, like Wallace and Bates in Leicester a generation before, collecting butterflies with his friend Robert Adkin. In middle age he found a kindred spirit in Ruskin whose literary style, together with Carlyle's, he adopted and adapted.

In 1865, after spending a year with an uncle who was chief warden of the convict settlement at Gibraltar, he entered the cramped quarters of the Royal College of Chemistry in Oxford Street. Since its amalgamation with the School of Mines in 1853, the College had become like a German university – at least for any student like Armstrong who was mature enough to exploit its potentials by sampling the affiliated courses at Jermyn Street. He later recorded his impressions in the essay on pre-Kensington science (*Kensington*) and in the Huxley Memorial Lecture (below). As a freelance, Armstrong also sampled the courses of Huxley, Ramsay, and Tyndall, as well as Frankland's in chemistry. Unaware of Huxley's reputation he 'had no call to be a hero-worshipper' (*C.*, 35 (1938), 3) and consequently he was unimpressed by Huxley's zoology teaching; and he diagnosed that Huxley was a poor teacher for introductory classes. One learned Huxley's opinions about an issue, but not 'how to form opinions of your own'. Only later did Armstrong learn of Huxley's 'pontifical importance in the teaching world' (*ibid.*, 4); certainly by the 1880s he had been influenced by his writings and had definitely set out to follow his example as a propagandist.

He was a registered student at the R.C.C. for only four terms; for late in 1866 Frankland paid him the compliment of taking him into his private laboratory. Given the minimum of help, Armstrong's task was to devise a new and accurate method for the determination of organic matter in water supplies. His technically-difficult solution worked, and it was published in 1868. He remarked later that 'there was no trace of the slave driver' in Frankland. 'Only those could work effectively with Frankland who needed little if any guidance; but at times he would step in and give invaluable advice or still more important assistance by coming to the worker's aid with his wonderful manipulative skill' (*Kensington*, 6). This skill had been largely self-acquired. Disadvantaged by illegitimacy, shyness, and a poor ability as a lecturer, Edward Frankland had been apprenticed to a Lancaster pharmacist for five years before he entered Playfair's London laboratory in 1845. Through the influence of the German chemist Hermann Kolbe he spent three months at Marburg in 1847 before joining John Tyndall as a science teacher at the extraordinary Quaker school, Queenwood College, Hampshire. Here he taught practical chemistry, botany, and geology, while Tyndall taught surveying, mathematics, and engineering physics. In 1848 Frankland returned to Marburg to study with Bunsen, and after obtaining his degree in 1849 he became the first Professor of Chemistry at the newly-opened Owens College, Manchester. Dissatisfied by life in the provinces, and by the elementary nature of the courses required at Owens, he moved to London in 1857 to teach at St Bartholomew's Hospital and the Royal Institution before succeeding to A.W. Hofmann's position at the R.C.C. in 1865. According to Armstrong, who adored Frankland:

Frankland was so thrown upon himself, he so developed the art of self-help, that he never learnt to order and use others sufficiently, which is the teacher's art; he kept counsel with himself . . . Frankland was a pattern worker to those who were privileged

to work for him; they gained lessons for life . . . His lectures were
clear, straightforward and logical and he took particular pains to
illustrate them by well-thought-out, practical demonstrations
(*J.S.C.I.* (1935), 464).

But Frankland did not merely mould Armstrong's career
by providing him with a solid chemical foundation, or
with a love of the practical, or by providing him with his
first research problem, or by packing him off to Germany.
For Frankland was also interested in science education.

In the 1860s, following the codification of physics by
the concepts of energy and entropy, chemistry by those
of valency and atomism, and biology by evolution, the
scientists themselves began to form an effective pressure
group, or groups, which urged a fuller appreciation of, and
a more systematic teaching of their interests.[2] At the
centre of this propaganda movement were the nine men
who together formed the X Club in 1854. The members,
most of whom examined for the Department of Science
and Art (D.S.A.), included the biologists T. H. Huxley,
J. Hooker, and J. Lubbock (Lord Avebury), the chemist
Frankland, the physicist Tyndall, the mathematician
T. A. Hirst, and the philosopher Herbert Spencer.[3] The
epicentre of their campaign was the Royal Institution
where Tyndall (and, among others, Faraday and Whewell)
had delivered the first broadside in a series of lectures in
1854. Spencer's remarkable essays on education, in which
science appeared as the universal panacea of education and
civilisation, belonged to the same period, and were collectively republished in 1861, a few years before the Clarendon Commissioners, primed by the arguments of a group
of scientists, which included Hooker and Faraday, urged
the adoption of science by the Public Schools. There
followed a decade's debate over the relative merits of
classics, mathematics, and science as formative elements
in 'Liberal Education'. The controversy, together with

the scientists' use of formal faculty psychology and the bogy of foreign economic achievement, interested many Broad Church clergymen like Kingsley, Farrar, and Wilson. Kingsley's lectures to the boys of Wellington College, with their emphasis on observation, were to be frequently quoted by Armstrong as authoritative arguments for practical science teaching (*S.M.*, 4, 7, 381). Farrar, then a teacher at Harrow, published his important *Essays on a Liberal Education* in 1867; one of the essays was by 'the Nestor of Science Masters', J. M. Wilson (1836–1931), then a young mathematics master who had deeply impressed the Clarendon Commissioners by his practical science classes at Rugby school. His curriculum, based on the science of common things, also impressed Farrar. At the British Association for the Advancement of Science meeting at Nottingham in 1866 the latter launched the first of its educational campaigns in the form of a committee, composed of himself, Wilson, Tyndall, and Huxley, 'to consider the best means of promoting scientific education in schools'. Its report issued in 1867 (which was presented to Parliament) distinguished scientific *information* from *training* (*B.A.R.*, 1867). This distinction, which the phrenologist and secular educationalist George Combe had called *positive instruction* and *instrumental instruction* (meaning the training of the phrenological faculties), was the antecedent of Armstrong's distinction between scientific *facts* and scientific *method*. The practical conclusion expressed by Farrar's committee was that there existed a common core of factual information which covered the laws and phenomena of everyday life and familiar experience, and which formed an essential part of everyone's knowledge. Here was the seed of the General Science campaign, Armstrong's and Gladstone's call for a science of everyday life, as well as Huxley's startlingly successful textbook *Physiography*.[4] On the other hand, the

Committee recommended special training in physics, chemistry, or biology in order to stimulate the dormant areas of the mind which were neglected by mathematics and classics teaching, i.e. powers of observation, classification, and induction.

Until the Elementary Education Act of 1870 most science teaching took place under the auspices of the D.S.A. Under the rigorous financial control of their examination results, such classes, whether in evening or day schools, tended to be non-practical, textbook-oriented and imbued by rote learning. Both Frankland and Huxley tried to stimulate practical science teaching by holding summer schools for science teachers during the 1870s, but the practical instruction they encouraged, and the practical textbooks which followed the wake, were of a manipulative and demonstrative character.

Farrar's report of 1867 also alerted the British Association and Gladstone's government to the needs of scientific instruction, and, together with the X Club's campaign for the 'endowment for research', led directly to the Devonshire Commission on Scientific Instruction and the Advancement of Science, which sat from 1871 to 1875. The Commission's sixth report, masterminded by Lockyer, and published in 1875, dealt with scientific education in schools and recommended that all Public and Endowed Schools should allot some six hours a week to science. The Commission also recommended the transfer of the Royal School of Mines, together with the R.C.C., to South Kensington. In 1881, following pressure from Huxley and Donnelly, the School of Mines was transformed into a Normal School for the training of science teachers. But it reverted to a pure science college, the Royal College of Science, after Huxley's retirement in 1885.

With the advent of the School Boards in 1870, science returned to the curriculum of the elementary schools, influenced by the Liberal Education controversy of the 1860s. The new complicated Code awarded grants to the upper standards of schools for certain optional or 'special' subjects, which included mechanics, animal physiology, botany, agriculture, physics, and chemistry. By 1882 the Code had been further modified to permit the teaching of elementary science, or geography, as optional *class* subjects above the first standard, while specific subjects like mechanics could still be taken from standards IV to VI. In practice the specific subjects were relatively unpopular (*Selleck*, 37–9), and elementary science fared badly against the competition of English and geography (W. J. Harrison, *I.C.E.*, ii, 119–20). Notable exceptions occurred in the schools governed by the School Boards of London, Liverpool, and Birmingham, where scientists like Huxley and J. H. Gladstone offered advice and active encouragement. Here the Boards developed coherent graded object lessons and developed the economically-successful method of peripatetic science demonstrations (*ibid.*, 145).

When Armstrong returned from Germany the students he faced had been subjected to the authoritarianism of teachers and books whose words related little to the practical things of life. His predecessors had successfully brought science to schools and colleges; but they had never presented unanimous views on how (in detail) science had to be taught, and how the curriculum had to be organised. It was here that Armstrong scored. But first we must see how he learned to appreciate scientific method.

Armstrong spent five semesters in Kolbe's laboratory at Leipzig. Because of his infamous lampoons and polemics against Kekulé and van't Hoff, Kolbe's reputation as a great teacher ('Try it! Try it!') and innovator of structural chemistry, was soon eclipsed, while the reputation of those he attacked 'thrived on the publicity'. Too often remembered for being on the wrong side, his role in the history of nineteenth-century chemistry still awaits proper assessment.[5] He wrote clearly and precisely and abhorred looseness of language. He expressed his own views forcibly and without bowing his knee to authority. The similarity to Armstrong is obvious; the latter himself recognised this as a compliment. Kolbe was an outstanding teacher in the German tradition of Liebig, Hofmann, and Bunsen, and despite the unfashionable character of his theoretical ideas, his laboratories never lacked students or research workers. He not merely reinforced his friend Frankland's tuition in experimental techniques but pushed Armstrong into the excitement of research into aromatic chemistry. Armstrong was left *selb-ständig*, able to walk alone (*R.I.C.*, 1924, 13). In addition, Armstrong's proneness towards a sharp tongue and a critical attitude towards scientific theories, whether in attack or defence, was a legacy from Leipzig. Frankland and Kolbe, then, made Armstrong a critical and passionate believer in self-education through laboratory research.

According to Armstrong his own interest in the practice of scientific method was originally literary – a surprising confession for one who had no faith in the traditional literary education. 'As a lad, I had read omnivorously and learnt not a little . . . I had, however, the definite feeling that something was wanting: I could not find any reference to "origins". I use the word advisedly, because the desire to know these things came in through using Trench's *Study of Words*, at school' (below, 61). The Irishman Richard Chenevix Trench (1807–86), poet, Professor of Divinity at King's College, London, and, from 1863, Archbishop of Dublin, appears at first sight a curious bedfellow for Armstrong until it is remembered that Trench was the philologist who popularised the scientific study of language in Great Britain and who founded the

scheme for the *Oxford English Dictionary* in 1867. His
Study of Words, first published in 1851, originated in
lectures he gave to schoolmasters and student teachers in
Winchester in 1845 'so that they shall learn to regard
language as one of the chiefest organs of their own education and that of others'.[6] The *Study*, which had reached
nineteen editions by the time of Trench's death, was
already a 'classic' school-prize type of book before Armstrong had reached school. Not surprisingly, it was an
intensely religious and moral work, and pre-Darwinian
in the *naïveté* of its natural theology, but written in a rich
prose whose beneficial influence on a reader cannot be
doubted. 'We could scarcely have a single lesson on the
growth of our English tongue, we could scarcely follow
up one of its significant words, without having unawares a
lesson in English history as well, without not merely falling
on some curious fact illustrative of our national life, but
learning also how the great heart which is beating at the
centre of that life was gradually shaped and moulded'
(Trench, *op. cit.*, 44). Although Trench discussed the
origins of new words, including scientific ones, the principal essay that engaged, or was related to, the concept of
method was concerned with the discovery of the relationship between words, especially between homonyms.

Armstrong first referred to the influence of Trench in
his paper on heurism for the Board of Education in 1898.
Subsequently, he frequently mentioned the way that he
felt Trench had made him 'critical and anxious to get
behind meanings' (below, 61). It was this influence, he
said, which prevented him from liking Huxley's didactic
approach. The origins of Armstrong's heurism, or his
stress on scientific method, clearly cannot be ascribed to
Trench alone. At the best Trench reinforced the lessons
learned at home from a father who used words carefully,
and helped lay the foundation for Armstrong's vigorous

prose style, which he later embellished with influences from Carlyle and Ruskin. As to method *per se*, Trench's thorough questioning of evidence was to be given scientific meaning by Frankland's and Kolbe's research methods and (if we again accept Armstrong's self-analysis) by a singularly meaningful legal experience.

Salicylic acid, which is found in plants of the *Spirea* genus (hence *aspirin*), was first synthesised by Kolbe in 1860 and shown by him (and others) to possess valuable properties as a food preservative, analgesic, and antifebrin. However, the cost of production was high until 1873 when Kolbe developed a cheaper and elegant commercial method of production which involved the carboxylation of sodium phenoxide. The process was patented in February 1874 and awarded to Kolbe's pupil Friedrich von Heyden, who was able to reduce the price of salicylic acid from thirteen shillings an ounce (1868) to 7s 6d per pound (1880). However, in November 1877 the London druggists Messrs Neustadt patented a virtually identical process whose only difference was the use of anhydrous sodium phenoxide. This patent was worked by Neustadt's German partners, the famous firm of Emanuel Merck of Darmstadt, the acid being imported and distributed by Neustadt. The aggrieved von Heyden was granted an injunction against Neustadt in 1879; the latter's appeal in February 1880 brought Armstrong into the witness box as a scientific expert for von Heyden. The appeal was dismissed in March 1880, the Court entirely believing 'what the scientific witness, Dr Armstrong, stated, that the discovery, the subject of the patent, took him entirely by surprise, although he had been a pupil of Kolbe's, and was conversant with what had been previously done by him in this matter' (*Law Times Report*, 42 (1880), 302).

Armstrong was tremendously impressed by this case, the Court atmosphere, the dialectic, the way plaintiff and defendant marshalled their respective arguments, and the clear, incisive manner in which judgement was delivered. 'The display of judicial method', he wrote later, 'the stringent examination and cross-examination of every particular, came to me as the acme of scientific treatment. I realised how far short we were from it in our ordinary treatment of our problems.'[7] This experience, he felt, had been a coping stone to his education. Scientific training had taught him to examine evidence and to ask questions about causes. Trench had caused him to worry about meaning. The patent action made him instead 'alive to the need of a searching cross-examination and judicial consideration of every item for and against a proposition' (below, 69). Facts were one thing, 'the methodical logical use of knowledge' which Armstrong called *scientific method* was another.[8]

On returning to England in 1870 Armstrong was appointed to help Augustus Matthiessen teach chemistry at St Bartholomew's Hospital. He coached students there for London University First M.B. examinations for twelve years 'with no little gain in experience' of students and the influence of examinations. At the end of 1870 he was appointed to succeed Frankland's great rival in water analysis, Alfred Wanklyn, at the London Institution. Housed though it was in a beautiful and elegant building, the London Institution was never as successful as its rival, the Royal Institution, and it was in continous financial distress from its foundation in 1805. Armstrong, who retired from the Institution in 1884, was the last of its scientific professors. It limped into the twentieth century, then in 1912 its premises were taken over by the University of London for the School of African and Asian Studies and no further members were elected; Armstrong lived to see the building demolished in 1936. His duties were fairly nominal – the delivery of evening lectures to artisans on 'analytical chemistry and the methods of original investigation'; but it gave him time for research in the Institution's small laboratory, and a sufficient salary to marry a Lewisham druggist's daughter, Frances Louisa Lavers, in 1877.

The students at the London Institution were very different in temperament from the medical students of St Bartholomew's. He was no longer tied by examination syllabuses; a release that left him free to devise methods of teaching that would develop the fundamentals of chemistry in a relevant way for the practical trades followed by members of his classes. Gradually he discovered ways for interesting his audiences by encouraging them to tackle problems experimentally in the confined and dusty Institution laboratory.

It was during Armstrong's period with the London Institution that Huxley published several essays on education, and began to criticise the wealthy City Guilds for their neglect of their historical role as technical educators. In 1878 a Committee of Livery Companies reported on technical education and recommended a practical plan for the creation of a central London institution which would serve as a model trade school. Eleven companies together financed this scheme, which became officially known as the City and Guilds of London Institute. Anxious to make an immediate start the Institute created two lectureships in applied chemistry and physics. In October 1879 Armstrong was appointed to the former on the basis of his experience at the London Institution (whose proprietors were all City men). The physics post was taken by the electrical engineer W.E. Ayrton (1847–1908), who had just returned from teaching in Japan. Temporary quarters were taken in the Cowper Street Schools, which already had a strong tradition of evening classes under the D.S.A. Courses began in November 1879.

Immediately Armstrong planned a new kind of chemistry course, beginning with elementary principles and familiar phenomena such as combustion, proceeding to pure and applied inorganic and organic chemistry, and concluding with a thorough outline of industrial chemistry; the whole scheme was to be illustrated by experiments (*Eyre*, 68). Ayrton had the advantage of teaching a new subject, electrical engineering; the method he adopted was practical, but in Armstrong's eyes too didactic. 'The student found himself in face of certain apparatus and the instructions he needed to carry through the verification of this or that theorem – Ohm's Law, for example' (below, 71). The students *did*, but with little call for mental effort on their part. Armstrong believed his own position to be different and more difficult. 'I had to deal with an age-old subject and put new life into old bones.' After a long struggle he persuaded Ayrton and the Council of the Institute to agree to have a composite building in which all the first-year subjects (mathematics, engineering drawing and elementary workshop practice, chemistry and physics) were common to all students; specialisation was deferred until the second year. There was an entrance examination, but no externally controlled examinations (*C.*, 30 (1933), 35–48; *Eyre*, 284–9).

The new building, known as Finsbury Technical College, was designed by E.C. Robins (d. 1890), who strongly supported the idea of general teaching and the method of teaching science by experiment (*Eyre*, 72–5). Subsequently Robins became the English expert on laboratory design and composed an influential treatise on laboratory and workshop architecture.[9] The new building at Finsbury was not completed until 1883; until then classes continued successfully at Cowper Street with up to 800 day and evening students.

Meanwhile, plans for a Central Institution, or Technical

University, of the City and Guilds of London Institute continued. A site was taken at South Kensington and the unfurnished building was opened in June 1884 to coincide with the start of the large International Health Exhibition at Kensington. Four professorships, of chemistry, engineering, mechanics and mathematics, and physics, were attached to this new college, and Armstrong, W. C. Unwin, O. Henrici, and Ayrton were appointed to them (*Eyre*, 84). Courses in mechanical, electrical, and chemical engineering began in January 1885, with the intention of providing a higher level of instruction than was possible at Finsbury for students who would probably attain responsible positions in industry or become technical teachers. Both Ayrton and Armstrong devised broad four-year courses, but these were trimmed to three years by the City and Guilds. Armstrong retained a common first-year heuristic chemistry course for all three streams of students, based upon the study of the conditions under which iron rusts, the atmosphere, the earth, chalk, and sea-water (*ibid.*, 289–96). But the Finsbury Plan whereby all students read a common course in the first year had to be abandoned. Unfortunately, the three-year chemistry course proved unpopular, and this phenomenon, coupled with a difficult administrative system and public allegations that the 'Central' was a white elephant, sometimes made Armstrong's life frustrating (*ibid.*, 94–102).

By 1901 the number of students reading applied chemistry (the term chemical engineering was disapproved by the authorities) was still static compared with the numbers taking electricity and mechanics; moreover, fifty per cent of those students who sat London University examinations in chemistry failed (*ibid.*, 146–50). Armstrong rightly blamed the attitude of industrialists towards chemistry for the small numbers, as well as the lower fees charged by other London colleges where chemistry was studied; he admitted, too, that the excess failure rate in external examinations was due to his department's emphasis on practical, as opposed to, bookwork. But, in terms of research output and honours gained by his former students, his department had more prestige than any other chemistry department in London. Nevertheless, there was an unpleasant implication that he was inefficient as a teacher.[10] The Central College had been recognised as an engineering college by the University of London in 1898. In 1906 the Haldane Committee produced a scheme whereby the independent work of the three colleges at South Kensington – the Royal School of Mines, the Royal College of Science, and the Central Institution – could be streamlined and co-ordinated. The result was the creation of the Imperial College of Science and Technology in 1907. Duplication and overlapping of courses were to be avoided henceforth; the Central College became a Department of Engineering. The result was inevitable, but none the less cruel when it came in 1911. Armstrong's chemistry department was abolished, to be replaced by that of the Royal College of Science, whose precursor had been his own school – Frankland's Royal College of Chemistry.

   Although aged sixty-three, and near retirement, Armstrong was bitterly disappointed by these events. 'The change was made without any of us being consulted', he complained. 'My course, which had proved to be of special service, was destroyed. Students were turned over to the tender mercies of the Royal College of Science, where they received the treatment meted out to students of professional chemistry. The Central engineering course lost its special value' (*Eyre*, 163). The interesting Finsbury Technical Plan fared little better. The general first-year course was abolished under the Directorship of S.P. Thompson; the College was undersupported financially by the Guilds, and closed quietly in 1925.

Despite many signs of bitterness, Armstrong's long years of retirement, from 1912 to 1937, were years of activity and enjoyment (*ibid.*, part IV). In fact he was able to continue work in the Royal College laboratories, winding down various research projects, until 1913, while later, laboratory accommodation was found for him at the R.C.S. Thirty scientific papers were published during his retirement, as well as an enormous output of minor essays, reviews, and letters. He became a master of the essay form, a delight to editors. He was 'always readable ... and usually amusing and vigorous, probably too vigorous to carry such conviction as might have been possible. His style was entirely unorthodox, a derivative of Carlyle and Armstrong, the latter predominating' (*J.S.C.I.*, 1937, 669). Some of Armstrong's titles were delicious appetisers, ranging from his speech to a girls' school entitled 'Silken Stockings', to the extravagantly titled 'First Epistle of Henry the Chemist to the Uesanians'. He travelled a good deal, regularly attended scientific and educational meetings, socialised with former students, absorbed himself in the affairs and needs of Christ's Hospital and the Lawes Agricultural Trust, proselytised for wholesome diets and the conservation of natural resources like coal, and supported British dyestuffs flamboyantly by wearing waistcoats of vivid hue. He died quietly on 13 July 1937, his thoughts engaged on a plan for a critical history of education in his lifetime of ninety years.

The International Conference on Education was held under the auspices of the International Health Exhibition in August 1884 in the newly-completed Central Institution. To Armstrong's disgust he, J. H. Gladstone, and Fleeming Jenkin were the only professional scientists to attend (*I.C.E.*, iv, 452). Armstrong's challenging paper on the teaching of natural science, which was delivered in the section on Technical Teaching under the chairmanship of Philip Magnus (below, 74), argued against specialisation and recommended practically-oriented instruction. All the participants seemed pleased by his ideas and with the Finsbury syllabus he described, but the principal discussion centred on their incompatibility with examinations. How would a school earn a grant if it followed Armstrong's practical course? Schoolteachers would not dare experiment for fear that the D.S.A. would not pay. In reply Armstrong's Welsh assistant at Finsbury, John Castell Evans, who was largely responsible for the practical everyday details of the first-year heuristic course,[11] commented that in his experience it could be done; students would still pass the examinations. He revealed that he and Armstrong had been engaged in teaching a class of boys from Cowper Street Middle Class School since his appointment at Finsbury in 1880 – probably the first experiments in the 'classroom situation' in the world. He had obtained good results in the special physical science examinations (i.e. light, sound, heat etc.), even though he had adopted an analogous programme of individual experimentation to that of Armstrong in chemistry, and had not slavishly followed the South Kensington syllabuses. 'If the system described by Dr Armstrong had a fair trial it would be found to be more advantageous, even in the matter of pounds, shillings, and pence, than the one which had been in use for years' (*I.C.E.*, ii, 90).

Nevertheless, despite this practical evidence, the conclusion of most speakers was that the system of payment by results made Armstrong's methods unworkable. Yet Armstrong's activities at the Educational Conference showed that he was no mere idealist. He spoke from experience; he had consulted teachers and headmasters, he had taught schoolchildren and students himself, he had studied examination syllabuses and timetables, he had developed new methods which worked at the London Institution and Finsbury College; he was poised to gain more experience at the new Central Institution and by training teachers himself.

Another forceful speaker at the Education Conference was John Miller Dow Meiklejohn (1836–1902), one of the most prolific of Victorian school textbook writers (*D.N.B.*). An Edinburgh graduate, his younger days were spent in the study of Kant and of languages. After some years as a private tutor in the Lake District he settled in London as a journalist and writer. In 1869 he issued *The English Method of Teaching to Read* with the collaboration of Adolph Sonnenschein. His reports as Assistant Commissioner for the Endowed Schools Commission for Scotland, to which he was appointed in 1874, brought him to the attention of Dr Bell's Trustees. They appointed him to the new Chair of the Theory, History, and Practice of Education of St Andrew's University in 1876. It was in this professorial capacity that he was invited to deliver a paper to the Education Conference on 5 August 1884, on the same day that Armstrong read his paper. A glance at the Conference programme shows that both men read their papers at the same time in different sections. Armstrong, therefore, despite later statements to the contrary, did not hear Meiklejohn's humorous and stimulating paper on 'Professorships and Lectureships on Education'. He probably first read a shortened version of the paper in the *Educational Times* in September, and was subsequently able to use the Conference *Proceedings* when they were published at the end of 1884.[12] Armstrong found Meiklejohn's essay 'eminently suggestive' because it reinforced his own conclusions about 'pupil-centred' teaching, or 'their *finding out*, instead of being merely told about things, (below, 111).

Meiklejohn's concern was with the purpose and function

of those professionally concerned with the 'science' of education – of those academics we should now call 'educationalists'. His paper was little more than a digest of his inaugural lecture at St Andrew's in 1876. Educationalists, he argued, had to make comparative studies of the growth of young minds (*sc.* intelligence), they had to study and teach the history of education, and, above all, they had to study the methods of education.

What is the permanent and universal condition of all *method*? It is that it is *heuristic*. Man is by nature a seeking, inquiring, and hunting animal; and the passion for hunting is the strongest passion in him. This view has its historic side; and it will be found that the best way, the truest method, that the individual can follow, is the path of research that has been taken and followed by whole races in past times.[13]

Such a natural heuristic method, which he traced back to Edmund Burke and Pestalozzi, was more healthy, more real, than the methodological diseases of encyclopaedism, second-hand teaching, the tyranny of books or of teaching over the heads of the young, or the didactic infamy of telling instead of teaching. Of course, Meiklejohn's interest was to argue, ironically, that the humanities teacher should borrow this scientific method. 'The heuristic method is the *only* method to be applied in the pure sciences; it is the best method in the teaching of the applied sciences; and it is *a* method in the study of those great works of art in language by the greatest minds which go by the general aim of literature' (below, 112).

According to Charles Browne, Meiklejohn first used the term heuristic in 1860 (*Browne*, 1). He certainly used it in his inaugural lecture as if it were familiar to his audience.[14] Earlier the word was used, privately at least, in 1860 by that inveterate neologiser William Whewell, while other usages noted by the *Oxford English Dictionary* suggest that the word arose in a philosophical context, perhaps that of

Kantian studies. However, there existed a definite educational precedent for the term 'heuristical method'. In
1848 an Inspector of Schools for the Manchester Church
Education Society named Ross published an interesting
Teacher's Manual of Method. He explained that there
were only two ways of imparting knowledge: 'it may be
more or less elicited or developed from elements previously
existing in the minds of the pupils' or 'it may be directly
and wholly imparted' (*Ross*, 66). The former method,
which was preferred since it was more interesting and the
pupils were active participants, was divisible into five
techniques: catechetical (teaching by Socratic questioning), elliptical (pupil supplies missing words), heuristical,
dokimastical (the proof of what is already imparted), and
dialogical (a dialogue between pupil and teacher as equals).
Ross apologised for the classical nature of these words
which he used, or introduced, in order to avoid circum-
locution. Ross's use of the heuristical method was, in fact,
far more restricted in its scope than Armstrong's phrase
heuristic method was to imply, and was closer to the notion
of exercise, as Ross's recommendation for homework employment revealed. He confined its use to the field of
mathematics in which 'the matter of instruction is generally presented in the form of precomposed [*sic*] questions,
whose solutions the pupil are required to find out' (*ibid.*,
92). Furthermore, worthy of Whewell himself, he subdivided the method into *analytico-* (e.g. in mathematics
and parsing) and *synthetico-heuristical methods* (e.g.
scrambled sentences, map-making from written information), the latter, of course, bearing a much greater resem-
blance to Armstrong's intentions since it required the
student to build up a conclusion from its elements.

Armstrong said that the term heuristic had still not
reached the dictionary in 1898 (below, 110). It is not clear
when he first employed it himself. His earliest printed use

seems to be in the title of his address to the International Conference on Technical Education, which was held at the Society of Arts in June 1897,[15] and in his essay for Frederick Spencer in the same year (below, 106). His Special Report on the Heuristic Method for the Board of Education in 1898, however, soon gave the term wide currency. By the time of Meiklejohn's death *heurism* was recognised as the war-cry of those who believed all teaching should be by means of carefully directed inquiry (e.g. W.M. Heller and E.G. Ingold, *Elementary Experimental Science*, 1905).

Heuristic methods, of course, are as old as scholarship. They are to be found recommended by Locke and Rousseau, and their English disciples at the Birmingham Lunar Society, Erasmus Darwin (*Female Education*), Thomas Day (*Sandford and Merton*), and Richard Lovell Edgeworth (*Practical Education*).[16] Armstrong's heurism embraced four intuitive theses. First, that what a child or student finds out for himself he remembers. Secondly, motivation and interest: if a student is interested and realises that something is worth learning he will do it more efficiently. Thirdly, but less clearly, the learning situation must be graded – children will learn certain things better at different ages. Fourthly, that if children keep a carefully written record of their findings this will help to correlate their mental and verbal understanding and relate a student's scientific awareness to his study of the English language. The whole emphasis was on *doing* in order to *understand*. Precisely what was learned was less important, at least in the first instance, than the method involved in learning, thinking, or finding out about something. From a modern viewpoint Armstrong seems to have been encouraging intuitive, rather than analytic, thought (J.S. Bruner, *The Process of Education*, Cambridge, Mass., 1966). Armstrong believed, as the history of science indicated, that once a person had learned the methods of experimentation he could continually use these techniques to 'find out', and so tirelessly acquire by his own efforts the mass of information which other teacher-centred systems of education forced into children by rote, demonstrations, and the exigences of examinations. How could he convince the teaching profession?

Ever since its foundation in 1831 the British Association for the Advancement of Science had been a valuable annual public platform for the announcement of new ideas or experimental work, or for the discussion and report of scientific enterprises. Papers on educational subjects were sometimes presented, especially in Section F, Economic Science and Statistics. As we have seen, a sound precedent for the discussion of science education had been created by Farrar's Committee of 1866. A second wave of discussions at the B.A. took place during the 1880s, following the Elementary Education Act, the creation of the School Boards, and the establishment of the New Revised Code. In 1879 the chemist and philanthropist John Hall Gladstone (1827–1902), who had been elected to the London School Board in 1873 (and effectively replaced Huxley who had resigned in 1872), succeeded in creating a B.A. watchdog committee on elementary schools under the auspices of Section F.[17]

In 1885 Armstrong was President of Section B, Chemistry, at Aberdeen. Over half of his address was devoted to education, and it was a signal that he intended to use the British Association as a propaganda machine for his ideas. In the summer of 1886, no doubt with the discussion of a 'rational system' of instruction in mind, Armstrong wrote to both Gladstone and the former school teacher W.A. Tilden to suggest that the subject of science teaching in schools be brought before Section F. Tilden replied that he had already tried to persuade William Crookes, President of the Chemical Section that year, to discuss the subject in Section B; but Crookes would 'not bite' (2 June 1886, *I.C.A.*). Gladstone welcomed the suggestion, but pointed out that plenty of opportunity for discussion did already exist whenever his elementary school's committee reported to the British Association (June 1886, *I.C.A.*). Significantly, at the Birmingham meeting, Armstrong was co-opted onto Gladstone's committee. However, its range of inquiry was limited to elementary schools, whereas Armstrong wanted to know the fate of science-teaching, especially chemistry, over the whole range of school education. In 1887, at the Manchester meeting, he succeeded in creating a committee to consider and report on 'the present methods adopted for teaching chemistry'.[18] The committee comprised the chemists Armstrong, Meldola, Smithells, Gladstone, W. J. Russell, A. G. Vernon Harcourt, Pattison Muir, and W. R. Dunstan (a pharmacist), and the chemistry school-teachers J. T. Dunn, Francis Jones, and W. A. Shenstone. The absence of Ramsay's name is noteworthy.

In December 1887 this committee circularised 500 headmasters and training college Principals asking them why they taught chemistry, what difficulties they experienced, and what teaching methods they found to be most efficient. Although there were only eighty-six replies the committee was able to compose an interesting report for the Bath meeting in 1888 (*B.A.R.*, 1888, 73–89). Chemistry, they found, was being taught both as a form of mental training and exercise and because of its applications in various walks of life. Teaching difficulties included expense, the low value put upon the subject compared with other subjects in the curriculum, the examination syllabuses, and the absence of good textbooks and qualified teachers; but, above all, there was a general difficulty over the lack of good laboratories. On method there was a surprising unanimity in the view that the subject should be taught experimentally; and a general feeling prevailed that too great an emphasis on qualitative analysis and manipulation was to be found in existing practical courses. The committee itself concluded that something 'should be done in the direction of promoting a more uniform and satisfactory treatment' of chemistry teaching (*ibid.*, 88). To this end, they promised to suggest new methods of teaching chemistry.

Impatient of further prolonged discussion, and brimfull with constructive ideas, Armstrong volunteered to produce some 'suggestions for a Course of Elementary Instruction in Elementary Science'. Such suggestions were presented at Leeds in 1889 (below, 90), strengthened by support from the other members of the committee, who observed:

It cannot be too strongly insisted that elementary physical science should be taught from the first as a branch of mental education, and not mainly as useful knowledge. It is a subject which, when taught with this object in view, is capable of developing mental faculties that are not aroused, and are frequently deadened, by the exclusive study of languages, history, and mathematics. In order that the study of physical science may effect this mental education, it is necessary that it should be employed to illustrate the scientific method in investigating nature, by means of observation, experiment, and reasoning with the aid of hypothesis; the learners should be put in the attitude of discoverers and should themselves be made to perform many of the experiments. The lessons ought to have reference to subjects which can be readily understood by children, and illustrations should be selected from objects and operations that are familiar to them in everyday life (*B.A.R.*, 1889, 228-9).

The historical antecedents of this formal statement in the debates of the 1860s are obvious, though a new element of self-experiment had been injected. The committee recognised that Armstrong's course was incompatible with existing examination syllabuses. It hoped for co-opera-

tion from the Examination Boards – and it was soon forth-
coming. To be effective the syllabus had to be started at
'an early age' and include every child within a school.
The course was cheap since little apparatus was required.
One small observation seemed impracticable. 'A teacher
should not be required to give practical instruction to
more than from fifteen to twenty pupils at one time,
although the classes at lectures and demonstrations might
be somewhat larger' (*ibid.*, 229). How, then, could the
method be used in undisciplined larger classes?

Armstrong's constructive suggestions in fact took the
form of a detailed syllabus and science curriculum from
the age of seven to sixteen. Their basis in his 1884 Finsbury syllabus can be clearly seen, but they had now a more
developed and 'more consistently logical form' as a result
of practical trials at Finsbury and the Central Institution,
and reports of successful object lessons at the London
Board schools. Armstrong's course was divided into six
stages, each of which stressed 'doing'. Object lessons –
real objects which were part of a normal child's experience
– formed the foundation stone for later studies and allowed
the introduction of geography and natural history. This
first stage approached the physiography of Huxley. Once
children had gained proficiency in elementary arithmetic,
they were ready for 'lessons in measurement', including
the use of the balance, the determination of relative
densities of common materials, and the measurement of
temperature. This second part of the syllabus, which led
into elementary physics and meteorology, was strongly
influenced by the experience of A. M. Worthington at
Clifton College, Bristol.[19]

In Stage III the physical and chemical effects of heat on
common substances (including foodstuffs) were studied,
accompanied by the inculcation of student note-taking.
The open-ended conclusion of this stage was supposed to

be that heat changes involved more than mere destructive effects. The problem of chemical change, which was entered into in more detail in Stage IV, swept away the traditional catalogue approach of elements, oxides, and salts. Armstrong recommended instead a concentric approach which began with the rusting of iron, led logically (by the detective's method) to the analysis of air and to the phenomenon of combustion and oxidation, and to the application of the concept of *analysis* to substances like chalk, the 'discovery' of carbon dioxide, sulphur dioxide and hydrogen, and, finally, to the concepts of acidity, basicity, and the element. Altogether thirteen problems were suggested which were 'so arranged as to constitute a well-defined sequence of steps to a sound understanding of the main principles of chemistry: at the same time their design and treatment [were] intended to inculcate a scientific attitude of mind' (*Eyre*, 270). The pupils were now in the possession of a fair knowledge of the basic substances of chemistry and their properties, and of the idea of composition. Most students would stop at this point. Those that continued could proceed to a more sophisticated quantitative study of substances, partly by lecture demonstrations (a point often ignored by heuristic extremists), partly by individual experimentation, until the basic laws of chemical combination and the technique of volumetric analysis were achieved. It is noticeable that Armstrong did not introduce the atomic theory, or chemical symbols and equations, until the final stage, which made a closer investigation of the physical properties of the three stages of matter. This attitude towards theory was fully in line with nineteenth-century attitudes towards the concept of atomism.[20]

Although Armstrong recommended that most of the experimental investigations should be made by the pupils themselves, he allowed that the course would still be valuable even if given entirely by demonstration. The complete course would be very time-consuming, as well as incompatible with existing examinations, he recognised. In a further amplificatory report at Leeds in 1890, 'Exercises Illustrative of an Elementary Course of Instruction in Experimental Science' (*S.M.*, 345–66), he discussed such difficulties. The criticism of time consumption would disappear if the fallacy that 'sufficient training in a scientific subject [could] be imparted in the course of a term or two' (*ibid.*, 346) were overcome; and if it were realised that his course was not meant to be entirely practical work. On class numbers, Armstrong suggested that ways could be found for sharing out practical work within lessons and in consecutive lessons by means of sets – already used by Worthington.[21] Even with only one such lesson a week, one teacher and his assistant could 'deal with 240 pupils or with half that number if each class had two lessons per week – a much better course'. The 'laboratory' did not need to be elaborate: a simple table for the balances, a waxed table or bench fitted with gas taps, a fume cupboard, sink, and a muffle furnace. The only expensive items of equipment needed were a set of good balances and weights. Six of these, sufficient for a large class, would cost about £18. He thought that the total cost of apparatus for several classes of twenty-four pupils would not be greater than £50, providing porcelain vessels and not platinum ones were used.[22]

Armstrong's syllabuses of 1889 and 1890 had attracted widespread attention by 1891 when he lectured the College of Preceptors on the 'Teaching of Scientific Method' (*E.T.*, 1891, 211; *S.M.*, 1,367). By then, he had forwarded heurism in two practical ways. In 1888 a Cambridge- and German-trained chemist named Charles Maddock Stuart (1857–1932) was appointed the first headmaster of St Dunstan's College, a new school at

Catford, close to Armstrong's home at Lewisham.[23]
Stuart was also a former pupil of Frankland's at the
R.C.C., and he had taught chemistry at Clifton College
whilst Worthington was developing his practical physics
course. After research with Fittig at Strasbourg, he became a science teacher in a school at Newcastle under
Lyme. Given the extraordinary appointment of a
scientist headmaster, his interest in local affairs, and the
fact that one of the school governors was an Hon. Secretary of the City and Guilds Institute, it is not surprising
that Armstrong should have quickly made himself known
to Stuart, and 'influenced him from the beginning'. He
soon became a 'staunch, practising advocate of heuristic
tenets' (*Eyre*, 113) and Armstrong was to rank him above
Sanderson as a headmaster (*The Times*, 28 November
1932).

Here was a way to overcome accusations of idealism and
impracticability, or personal unfamiliarity with school-
teaching. Together Armstrong and Stuart, assisted practically by W. M. Heller (a former Central student), put the
heuristic system into operation at St Dunstan's, and gained
first-hand experience of the difficulties. The method was
soon extended to elementary mathematics and geological
geography (*Eyre*, 266), and eventually to manual work in
wood and metal. The success of this method of teaching
in a school environment encouraged Armstrong to enlarge
the scope of the attack in a second way through the training of teachers. Already in 1887 he had lectured on
chemistry to teachers in Public Elementary Schools. In
1896 he was given permission to hold Saturday morning
sessions for London science teachers at the Central
Institution. Nearly 200 teachers attended the first two
sessions, and the course was repeated over the next three
years (*ibid.*, 135). Among those who attended were several
of Armstrong's former students who had become teachers:

Grace Heath, a science mistress at the North London Collegiate School; L. Edna Walter, who eventually became an H.M.I.; and an Oxford graduate named Hugh Gordon. Gordon began research on organic chemistry with Armstrong in 1887, but soon found his educational research and his campaign more interesting. In 1891, after he had held information classes for teachers in the Surrey Council schools, he was appointed a peripatetic science demonstrator in mechanics for the London School Board. Encouraged by Armstrong, who longed to carry 'the war into the camp of elementary education' (*N.*, 50 (1894), 632), and by Gladstone, he began to hold training sessions in heuristic methods in a deserted rice mill at Whitechapel. These sessions, which were continued by Gordon and by his successor W. M. Heller in 1894, were well publicised. Thus Armstrong's introductory talk to teachers of Tower Hamlets and Hackney, which was given at the Berners Street Board School in October 1894, reached the pages of *Nature* (*ibid.*, 631–4). Unfortunately, when Heller left his peripatetic employment in 1897, three years after Gladstone's retirement from the London School Board, the latter failed to continue the system. On the other hand, the methods learned were transplanted to Ireland on the recommendation of the Irish Commission on Manual and Practical Instruction in Primary Schools. The subject 'General Elementary Science' became a compulsory part of Irish education, with Heller as its chief organiser.

Characteristically, Armstrong felt that Gordon's greatest achievement as a teacher was not so much his 'marvellous success, [as] his introduction of a proper balance' into schools (*ibid.*, 632), compared with the poor 'four shilling' affair recommended by Worthington. In 1893 Gordon published an *Elementary Course of Practical Science* in the excellent Macmillan Science Primer series edited by Roscoe. This was the outcome of the syllabus he had enforced in fifteen London Board schools between 1891 and 1893, but based originally on Armstrong's B.A. syllabus. Gordon's syllabus was accepted by the Education Department from 1893; while the rival D.S.A. agreed that preparation for their examinations should favour experimental work. Gordon's book was the first of many to adopt this syllabus. He claimed that the method of teaching 'should be that of suggestion combined with a minimum of demonstration – that of asking questions, not of answering them' (*op. cit.*, xv). Teachers should give lessons of forty minutes at least twice a week, and the pupils, say six at a time, should be required to perform experiments before the others. Gordon's book was designed to be read by the pupils themselves and skilfully interleaved interest items from newspapers on weight standards or meteorology in order to show the relevance of the experimental work.

By 1898, when Heller became Headmaster of the Municipal Technical School in Birmingham, over forty Schools in Tower Hamlets and Hackney had adopted the Armstrong–Gordon–Heller elementary science course (*S.R.*, ii (1898), 430). By then, too, the cause of heurism had been widened nationally, through the interest of the Incorporated Association of Headmasters, which had appointed a committee on science teaching to consider a syllabus which would be suitable for both boys and girls. Needless to say, since Armstrong was a member of the committee, the Headmaster's syllabus, which was adopted and published in 1896, was closely modelled on the B.A.s course of practical work (*N.*, 51 (1895), 464–7). The same committee consulted the Oxford and Cambridge Local Examination Boards in 1895, with the effect that the syllabus was approved for examination purposes, as well as for the award of scholarships and exhibitions offered by County Councils. (Whether the examination boards really understood the point of heurism was another matter, thought Armstrong.) Armstrong could also note with approval Professor Marshall Ward's concoction of an experimental natural history course in 1895. Later, in 1903, L. C. Miall devised a B.A. syllabus beginning with the bean seed, of which the germination and response to light and nutritive salts were to be experimentally investigated.[24]

Christ's Hospital, an ancient endowed school situated in Greyfriars, London, was distinguished for teaching mathematics. In 1891 the Charity Commissioners recommended that its Council of Almoners should move the school from Newgate Street to a new site, and introduce modern science teaching throughout the school. In 1896 Armstrong was made the Royal Society's representative, and, following his success in remoulding St Dunstan's College, it proved a wonderful opportunity for further educational experiments. Eventually after arguments, in which Armstrong was involved, the Almoners purchased an estate of 1,500 acres near Horsham in Sussex, and the country move was made in May 1902 (*Browne*, 9). Design of the buildings was placed in the hands of the architect of the South Kensington Museums and Science buildings, Aston Webb (1849–1930) and his partner Ingress Bell, who took Armstrong's advice (and *inter alia* Charles Browne's) throughout on the design of the science building.[25] Indeed, Armstrong's 'knowledge and advice were freely exercised' (*Eyre*, 122) during the forty years of his governorship. The teaching of science in the school was placed on an equal level with religious and literary studies; inevitably, it was Armstrong who devised the science syllabus. Later, a '*virus heuristicum Armstrongii*' spread to other subjects like geography, languages, and history (W. H. Fyfe, *S.S.R.*, 19 (1937), 1–2).

Armstrong had seven children who survived to adulthood. By 1898 his eldest son, Edward Frankland (*sic*) had passed through St Dunstan's and the Central Institution and was about to study chemistry in Germany; Clifford, who had received an identical education, was set to become an engineer; two daughters Edith and Annie had received a conventional education from a family governess and were destined for marriage; which left the three youngest children, Richard (Robin), who had just begun school at St Dunstan's, Nora, and Harold. They were at this time aged twelve, ten, and eight, and were conveniently sound materials for a part-time educational experiment on how to develop age-graded elementary science concepts in young children. Armstrong described their adventures, with showmanship and pride, at a conference of science teachers in 1900.[26]

At Christmas in 1897 he had given the youngest child a storybook entitled *The Monkey that would not Kill*.[27] In reading this story together:

they came across the statement that the monkey was thrown into the sea, tied to a stone which he could not lift – and that while under water he was able to lift the stone and walk to the shore, *because the stone was lighter than in air*. When the children asked if this could have been the case, they were advised to try for themselves. A balance being at hand and knowing how to weigh, they weighed a heavy stone in air and in water and so discovered that the statement in the storybook *was* true. It was then agreed to continue the work and that each child should write an account in copper-plate style, describing what was done (*S.M.*, 394–5).

These charming notebooks, which were kept from January 1898 until July 1901, fortunately still survive and their contents have been partially described by Browne and Eyre.[28] Much of their fascination lies in seeing how each child tackled the problems raised in a different way. What Armstrong succeeded in showing was that young children could approach definite problems as detectives and be led to important generalisations and concepts like *average*, *proportion*, *percentage*, *density*, *law*, or *accuracy*, and to develop techniques of manipulation, laboratory cleanliness, and mathematics – in particular graphical work – merely through the study of a common substance like water. Later, in 1906, he reported to the British Association on ways in which mathematics teaching could be correlated with other work in elementary schools by the use of shapes and patterns, or games involving children's ages (*S.M.*, 472–9).

The weekend sessions were sometimes witnessed by Charles E. Browne, a chemistry student and demonstrator of Armstrong's who had left the Central Institution to teach school science at the Robert Gordon College, Aberdeen in 1898. He returned to London in 1899, at the invitation of Armstrong, to become science master at Christ's Hospital. Before the move to Horsham, Browne taught science in a disused dormitory of the school, and it was here that he adapted Armstrong's heuristic ideas to the needs of school classes of fifty pupils.[29] 'Practical work by individual pupils became the accepted basis of the school science work throughout the school in all its grades' (*Browne*, 14). Pupils worked in pairs on a series of related problems, the results were tabulated and discussed by pupils and teacher and recorded in individual notebooks. By 1907, the scheme had worked so well that Armstrong was able to turn his attention to the provision of a manual workshop for metal and woodwork. However, in 1908 heuristic methods had to be drastically curtailed when the Board of Education forced the school to use the 'School Certificate' examination system as a criterion of its proficiency. Browne compromised by introducing periods of heuristic activity to fertilise the rest of the scientific teaching; these methods were continued at the school by John Bradley and Gordon Van Praagh, and, together with American project methods, were the indirect antecedents of the Nuffield Foundation's science teaching projects of the 1950s.[30]

During the 1890s the institutionalisation of heuristic methods was aided in an unexpected way. Fears of economic depression and international trade competition were continually expressed by scientists and enlightened industrialists from 1867 onwards. Following the Samuelson Commission on Technical Education, which heard evidence between 1882 and 1884, the chemist Henry Roscoe, together with Huxley, founded the National Association for the Promotion of Technical Education. The purpose was to lobby industrialists and Parliament to give local authorities rating powers to create facilities for technical education. Passage of the Local Government Act in 1888 made this possible; and in 1889 the new local councils were empowered to levy a penny rate for technical education. The curricula were to be controlled by the D.S.A. Fortuitously, these powers coincided with the temperance movement's successful appeal to tax spirits. In 1890 a Customs and Excise Tax was allotted to local authorities, who used it (and usually not the rates) to build laboratories and lecture rooms in the knowledge that science teaching gained South Kensington grants. In this way Armstrong's heuristic campaign was complemented financially and architecturally by the new buildings and laboratories of the 'secondary' schools and Technical Colleges. Practical science teaching on a wide scale became possible (A. Sutcliffe, *S.S.R.*, 11 (1929), 81–90).

Thus, when Armstrong spoke as President of the new Section L of the British Association in 1902 – the Education Section which he had forced the Association to accept in 1900 – he could survey with pride the success of the heuristic campaign: a corps of heuristic teachers, Christ's Hospital and its demonstration that conviction and skill solved the difficulty of large classes, 1,165 school laboratories throughout Great Britain (W. Abney, *B.A.R.*, 1903, 875), Domestic Science taught in girls' schools, and a new enthusiasm for practical technical education. Not that Armstrong was complacent. He castigated the English lack of imagination, the state of military education, examinations, and spoke of the danger of textbooks (*S.M.*, 35–96). Indeed, complacency would have been misplaced, for as we have seen, the growth of heurism was pruned at Horsham in 1908; by 1918 it could be said that 'in many schools more time is spent in laboratory work than the results obtained can justify' (*Thomson*, §42).

What were the roots of opposition? Heurism met with two kinds of temporal criticism: criticism prior to 1900 which was based upon the prediction of disasters and impracticability, and often based upon a superficial knowledge of Armstrong's syllabuses; and criticism in the twentieth century based upon hindsight which was much more objective and constructive.

Until 1884 Armstrong was known only as a chemist. It was by no means unusual for a chemist, or other scientists, to take an interest in education – the activities of Gladstone and Roscoe readily spring to mind. But since Armstrong was at the peak of his research career between 1880 and 1900, inevitably some of his friends and colleagues, as well as his family, felt that he gave up too much time to the cause of improved teaching, and this to the neglect of his chemistry. However, if one examines his research output during the years in which the heuristic campaign was at its height, there is no evidence that science was neglected. In fact he published well over 150 papers in this period, on such subjects as the nature of chemical change, a theory of residual affinity, naphthalene chemistry, as well as powerful criticisms of the new ionic theory. Admittedly, many of these papers were joint efforts, but he was no absentee collaborator (*C.*, 35 (1938), 68). Yet sheer output may mask the real point of this 'advice', for both friends and critics were perhaps thinking more of the quality of Armstrong's output, and especially of his trenchant criticism of the ionic theory which he began in the same decade as heurism.[31] His Kolbe-like invective made him many enemies, especially amongst the young school of physical chemists whose intellectual leader in England was William Ramsay. In 1894 Ramsay began his famous joint work with Lord Rayleigh which led to the discovery of argon. Rayleigh's colleague at the Royal Institution, where he was Professor of National Philosophy, was James Dewar – a difficult man whose one and only deep friendship was with Armstrong. It seemed incredible to many scientists, including Armstrong, that following the analysis of air at the end of the eighteenth century there could still be an undiscovered constituent. During Armstrong's Presidency of the Chemical Society from 1893 to 1895 he continually voiced Dewar's criticism that if the unknown gas existed Dewar would have found it in his technically-brilliant liquefaction of air. By January 1895, however, Armstrong had grudgingly admitted the existence of argon.

This was not the end of the matter. In 1897 Dewar was proposed as President of the Chemical Society, and Ramsay was forwarded as a rival candidate. After a campaign bristling with sarcasm by Armstrong, Dewar was elected. Armstrong never forgave Ramsay and under the thin disguise of '*Suum Cuique*' he poured scorn on Ramsay's work on the rare gases. In Armstrong's defence it can only be pointed out that the pages of *Chemical News* were continually filled with spurious reports of new elements; Armstrong's iconoclasm was in the spirit of Bacon's caution and Kolbe's scepticism. Unfortunately, in this instance events soon showed that Armstrong's caution was mistaken, and his attitude excessively rude and intolerant. It was easy for some to conclude that he had 'bees in his bonnet' and that his educational side-tracking had impaired his judgement.

Not surprisingly Ramsay did not fully applaud Armstrong's heuristic notions. In three lectures to the College of Preceptors in March 1891, he analysed the B.A. syllabus in some detail. Its lessons on measurement (Stage II) were devoid of interest unless given by gifted teachers, and the *information* to be garnered from this part of the course was desultory. The quantitative stage (v) was:

unsuited to the capacity of an ordinary class . . . the conclusions to be drawn are those which it has taken men of genius some 150 years to deduce, and it is not to be expected that an average schoolboy should make out such deductions for himself. Either he must be told, or he will read ahead . . . Children have small powers of reasoning; and it is inadvisable to set them problems in advance of their powers. Again, the difficulty of securing teachers competent to put such a scheme in practice would be unsurmountable (*E.T.*, 44 (1891), 228).

Ramsay's difference from Armstrong's approach was succinctly summarised by him:

I believe in facts; and I believe that the basis of theory is not grasped until the facts on which they rest have been learned (*ibid.*, 273).

But in 1891 Ramsay's views seemed to the progressive Armstrong to be reactionary and imbued with a perverse inability to understand the importance of training by scientific method. Yet, it remains true that many heuristic disciples did emphasise method as opposed to content – rather as contemporary nutritionists failed to discover vitamins because they emphasised the energy value of foodstuffs rather than the foods themselves.

Entrenched in the argument of both the older 'instrumental' education of the Codes and of the new 'practical' education was faculty psychology. For Armstrong, teaching the physical sciences would 'develop a side of the human intellect which . . . is left uncultivated even after the most careful mathematical and literary training: the faculty of observing and reasoning from observation and experiment' (below, 75, 91). Faculty psychology – the idea that the mind could be analysed in terms of various powers or faculties – originated in Greek philosophy. It seemed to gain powerful empirical support by the clinical observations of Gall and Spurzheim at the beginning of the nineteenth century – observations whose social and educational implications were developed in the phrenological movement by George Combe. Although the complex multiplication of entities by the British phrenologists, and its debasement by mesmerism and occultism, led to the discredit of phrenology, the phrenologists' belief that full development of the faculties, or organs, of imagination, judgement, reasoning, perception, and memory, (and a host of others) depended upon a person's environment and training, continued to be a useful educational way of justifying a particular curriculum throughout the nineteenth century. By formally training one faculty, or a part of it, it was claimed that the whole was improved for future use in any situation. Although the theoretical justification of the instrumentary education's emphasis on the three R's was faculty psychology, this was largely an afterthought. The need to teach reading, writing, and arithmetic was self-evident without deduction from theoretical faculties (*Selleck*, chap. 2). Yet so firmly entrenched was faculty psychology 'that a substantial group of the new educationalists, concerned to introduce extensive reforms in both the methods and the curriculum, were forced to argue their case on the basis of faculty psychology' (*ibid.*, 45–6). The unquestioned assumption made by reformers like Armstrong (on top of the unquestioned acceptance of faculties and their trainability) was that training could be transferred. Heuristic methods trained the faculties 'of thoughtfulness and power of seeing; accuracy of thought, of word, and of deed' (*S.M.*, 196). Outside school these attuned faculties would respond not merely to special scientific stimuli, but to the general stimuli of everyday life and work.

Such a theoretical justification for heurism was fated to be overtaken by the development of Hebartianism on the one hand, and of experimental psychology on the other. To both Armstrong at first turned a blind eye. Since the Herbartians emphasised the role of the teacher in moulding the child, and stressed the significance of books and literary studies, conflict with the practical educationalists was inevitable. For the remainder of his life, from 1900 to 1937, Armstrong was to thunder against the revival of the literary cult (*R.I.C.*, 1924, 10), and reserve the more vitriolic portions of his extensive vocabulary for psychologists. In fact, of course, formal training continued to be used in the practical arguments of educationalists and teachers; and in the end, during the last decade of Armstrong's life, psychologists grudgingly admitted that the doctrine of formal training held an element of truth which traditionally had been presented in a psychologically invalid manner (C. Burt, *S.S.R.*, 21 (1939), 653–4). A person's capacities were improved by formal training, but the transfer of capacities only occurred in a limited way between related fields. This admission was to help the revival of heurism in the 1930s.

Many teachers' organisations and pressure groups emerged between 1870 and 1910. The Mathematics Association which was founded in 1897 to improve mathematics teaching in schools is a good example. It drew on the experience of its forerunner, the Association for the Improvement of Geometrical Teaching, which had been founded by Hirst and Wilson in 1871 to help abolish

Euclid and teach geometry in a more practical manner. In 1900, in order to counteract their feeling of loneliness in public schools where classics were snobbishly thought to be superior to the sciences, the Association of Public School Science Masters was founded. Women teachers followed in 1912 with their own association. In 1919 the A.P.S.S.M. opened its ranks to other secondary school science teachers under the title Science Masters Association, and began the important journal *School Science Review* on the model of the *Mathematical Gazette* of the Mathematics Association. Since their foundations these professional organisations have played an effective role in pressurising for improved syllabuses and curricula, better and fairer examinations, and laboratory facilities. In 1963, in the wake of Nuffield enthusiasm, men and women teachers combined forces in the pressure group, the Association for Science Education.

The A.P.S.S.M. was originally conceived by four Eton science masters, T. C. Porter, W. D. Eggar, M. D. Hill, and H. de Havilland, in 1900. They held their first meeting in London in 1901 under the Chairmanship of Ostwald H. Latter, a master at Charterhouse, with Sir Henry Roscoe (not Armstrong, who nevertheless welcomed the organisation) as their first President. One of Latter's pupils was Archer Vassall, who taught at Harrow (*S.R.*, 6 (1900), 257–65). Latter, Hill and Vassall were the leaders of the A.P.S.S.M. and instrumental in getting biology taught in public schools, the momentum of which led to the 'General Science' movement in secondary schools (*S.S.R.*, 30 (1949), 244). It was Vassall who made the A.P.S.S.M. aware of the defects in faculty psychology, from which he concluded that schools must cultivate wider areas of knowledge and interest, and pay more attention to content and subject matter. However, Armstrong refused to accept the experimental findings which were the basis for Vassall's inferences (*N.*, 86 (1912), 394).

Although Armstrong's aims were achieved positively in a few schools, and (at a more advanced level) at his own Central Institution, his ideals were often debased into a heavy emphasis upon physical measurement and the physical sciences. The Ministerial code of 1904 had directed that instruction was to be given practically in two unspecified sciences. In the event this came to mean physics and chemistry; astronomy was too esoteric; anatomy and physiology too indelicate or bound up with the ethical problem of vivisection; and geology was still identified with religious controversy. Armstrong had always urged syllabuses based upon a science of everyday life which would include elements of astronomy, geology, and biology, besides physics and chemistry; but in many hands the enthusiastic probing for the means of inculcating 'scientific method' left pupils with very little factual knowledge and a depressed scientific vocabulary. Dissatisfaction with this state of affairs found an outlet through the A.P.S.S.M. and the British Association's educational section.

The trade depressions of the 1880s demonstrated to many scientists, especially chemists, that an industrial war could only be won if British industry and education altered radically. Fear of the industrial prowess of Germany, Japan, and America, coupled with the inefficient conduct of the Boer War and its revelations of educational and physical malnutrition, invited national comparisons. Armstrong was no exception; indeed, as a German-trained chemist, and as a visitor to America, he succeeded in using international comparisons with authority and without overstatement. He recognised that civilisation had been changed by scientific discovery and the application of science to industry; the language of practical science had to be taught in schools.

But the panic comparisons with German institutions

instanced by Sadler's *Secondary Education in Germany* (1902) and the Report by the London Technical Education Board's sub-committee on the Application of Science to Industry (1902), and his own contribution to the Mosely Report (1904), did not blindfold Armstrong to the dangers of copying foreign models.

Although as a member of the Mosely Commission he found much to praise in the standard of buildings, organisation, and equipment of American schools, and a praiseworthy 'absolute belief in the value of education both to the community at large, and to agriculture, commerce, manufacturers, and the service of the state', Armstrong was contemptuous of all American teaching methods except in medicine and manual training (M. C. Lupton, *Vocational Aspect*, 16 (1964), 36–49). His biggest criticism was the feminisation of American youth through coeducation and the prevalence of female teachers. He feared that coeducation would sap virility, as the late marriages and low reproductive rate of American graduates seemed to indicate. Women teachers were of historically-proven unoriginality: 'Those who have taught women students are one and all in agreement that, although close workers and most faithful and accurate observers, yet, with the rarest exceptions, they are incapable of doing independent original work' (below, 130). Such views were, of course, typically 'Victorian'. They were shared by all members of the commission with the notable exception of Ayrton, whose strange second wife was a mathematician (*N.*, 112 (1923) 800, 865). What were Armstrong's views on female education and science?

Women's place was in the home; hence her training had to enhance femininity, not destroy it. Its emphasis was to be on domestic science and household chemistry. The independence of women which had developed in his lifetime was superficial and unreal. 'She is more and more making herself the tool and slave of man, by undertaking work that is so monstrous and mechanical that he will not submit to it' (*J. Education*, June 1934). Women teachers should be married: 'the sexless creatures who too often engage in the vain task of training our daughters in the present days of higher education are a real danger to society' (*Cardiff*, 10). He remained suspicious of the female teacher all his life, and his son commented: 'He had little interest in the higher education of women, holding the conservative view that every woman should be a cook' (*J.S.C.I.*, 60 (1941), 84). Nevertheless, it must be said that Armstrong did all he could to promote the teaching of Domestic Science to girls, as a subject which bore directly on their future occupation. Women deserved to be taught methods of accurate thought for the successful management of the household (*S.M.*, 400–21).

When war came in 1914 Armstrong was overseas on a tour of the Far East. When he returned he engaged immediately in offering unsolicited advice on how chemical products, especially dyestuffs which had been imported from Germany, could be obtained. He also played his part in the war mania by seeking the resignation of Fellows of German extraction from learned societies. Education was temporarily forgotten. Consequently, he played no role in the 'Science for All' campaign mounted by a few teachers in the A.P.S.S.M., led by M.D. Hill, which aimed to further the claims of a more general kind of science teaching in 1915. On 2 February 1916 *The Times* published a letter from the A.P.S.S.M. blaming the state of the war on the neglect of science in British education. The letter soon led to the formation of 'The Neglect of Science Committee' whose most forceful members were the biologist E.R. Lankester, V.S. Bryant of Wellington School, and Gregory, a former laboratory assistant of Worthington's, textbook writer, staff writer for *Nature*, and editor of *School World* (W.H.G. Armytage, *Sir Richard Gregory*, 1957). Meanwhile, the A.P.S.S.M. had compiled a humanising syllabus entitled *Science for All* which effectively advocated what was soon afterwards called 'General Science'. This, together with the resolutions on the scientific curriculum from the 'Neglect' committee, were presented to 'The Committee Apointed by the Prime Minister to Enquire into the Position of Natural Science in the Educational System of Great Britain', which was appointed in August 1916 under the Chairmanship of the physicist J.J. Thomson. Simultaneously Gregory persuaded the British Association to set up another committee on science in the secondary schools, which was concerned with the essential place of science in general education. Armstrong, Sanderson, Vassall, and the dying Worthington served on this committee which reported in 1917 in time to be noticed by the Thomson team (*B.A.R.*, 1917, 123–207).

The pamphlet *Science for All*, which received wide distribution after the war through publication in C.L. Bryant's *School Science Review*,[32] was largely the work of Eggar of Eton, Oldham, and Vassall. Later it was thought to have been written deliberately in opposition to heurism, but this was denied by Bryant.

Indeed, we welcomed his campaign in so far as it supported our claims for more time and equipment for practical work in the schools, but we thought that the dear old man was too insistent on one method of teaching; we did not see why every child should walk around Ireland before he could believe it was an island. It fell to my lot to tell him so. He didn't like it, nor did I; but we remained friends all the same. *Science for All* was neither for nor against Armstrong . . . It just happened that the pamphlet was compiled at a time when relations between us were a bit strained (*S.S.R.*, 32 (1950–1), 143–4).

The strain was evidently over the A.P.S.S.M.s acceptance of the discreditability of faculty psychology, their belief that heurism needed to be tempered with a more informative approach, and, above all, their view that biology should share equally with the physical sciences and not form a lame coda to a science syllabus. Specialisation was bad – science was to be taught as part of the general education of everyone and not as if it was to be the vocation of everyone but a few specialists. Science had to appeal to the *imagination* as well as to the reason; this was something that 'the skilfully articulated skeleton of heurism' could not do. *Science for All* included a tentative syllabus of topics in which biology figured prominently, and which moved from cosmology to the gramophone. Complete freedom was left to the teacher to decide on the precise content and method, but in so far as the syllabus was more extensive than any proposed before, proponents of general science inevitably tended to favour teacher demonstrations rather than individual pupil experiments.

Gregory's British Association Committee reached similar conclusions which it saw as embracing the original aims of Farrar's Committee of 1866. The most interesting part of its unanimous report concerned the method of science teaching, for it revealed that Armstrong accepted the fallibility of faculty psychology as well as the criticism of form and content in many heuristic syllabuses. The view had gained ground, they reported, that 'all subjects, in different ways and to different degrees, can be made to give a training in scientific method'. However, if it were admitted that the sole task of a science teacher was to train pupils in scientific method and that this method was common to all well-conducted intellectual inquiries, there would be no need for special science teachers! 'This paradoxical conclusion depends upon the assumption that the method of scientific investigation can be regarded as separable from the matter, which is not correct ... No one ought to expect a training in scientific method acquired in one field of inquiry to be transferable to – that is, to guarantee competence in – a field substantially different from the former' (*B.A.R.*, 1917, 134). To Armstrong's disgust, Thomson was to take such an argument as evidence of the fallibility of heurism.

Despite the inflation of the cost of laboratory apparatus, the Committee stressed the unique value of laboratory work (*ibid.*, 137; *S.S.R.*, February 1920). It brought a pupil 'into direct contact with reality through his own senses and his own manipulation', and tested his reasoning powers in ways that the best manual training could not. But should laboratory work be by the subject-method (demonstration exercise) or problem-method (heurism)? The latter method, they felt was not intended, 'as is sometimes supposed, to make pupils discover for themselves laws and principles previously unknown to them, though to some extent this can be done, but rather to provide a continuous thread of reasoning for the practical work and a definite purpose for whatever is undertaken' (*B.A.R.*, 1917, 139). The method was acknowledged as difficult; freedom to use methods independently of external examinations was needed. Unfortunately, however, there had been a tendency for practical work to limit the scope of science courses. 'Increased attention to laboratory exercises has . . . often been associated with a very restricted acquaintance with the world of science. The tendency has been to make all teaching a matter of measurement, to the neglect of the human aspects of the pursuit of natural knowledge.' This ironic effect of Armstrong's success – making content 'narrow and special rather than broad and catholic' – was not lost on Thomson. Finally, Gregory's committee was concerned with the human aspects of science, and, no doubt urged by Gregory and Sanderson, they recommended lessons in the history of science and the discussion of modern scientific issues in schools. At all times scientific instruction was to be related to the affairs of everyday life. Thomson also appreciated this point. Syllabuses recommended by Vassall, Sanderson (Oundle), T. Percy Nunn, and Armstrong (a course on practical food studies) were also reproduced. All the courses included elements from biology as the science which most closely concerned human life.

Thomson's committee, upon which schoolteachers were not represented, reported in 1918. All the evidence presented to them had suggested that school science courses had become too narrow, both because of the undue emphasis on physics and chemistry, and the undue restriction of subject matter. 'Insistence on the view that experiments by the class must always be preferred to demonstration experiments leads to great waste of time', concluded Thomson.

Much of this waste of time is due to a conscientious desire of the teachers to encourage the spirit of inquiry by following the so-called heuristic method; the pupils are supposed to discover by their own experiments, with little or no suggestion from the teacher, the solutions of problems set to them or of problems which they themselves suggest. The spirit of inquiry should run through the whole of the scientific work, and everything should be done to encourage it, but it seems clear that the heuristic method can never be the main method by which the pupil acquires scientific training and knowledge. He cannot expect to rediscover in his school hours all that he may fairly be expected to know; to insist that he should try is to waste his time and his opportunities. (*Ibid.*)

Here was a caricature of Armstrong's intentions. For him heurism meant 'directed inquiry', with the teacher playing a discrete, but positive, role. The method was not meant to be the means by which stores of information were acquired, nor was it to replace entirely other methods of instruction and learning. But even though Thomson did not include these castigations in his important official recommendations, the damage was done.

Not surprisingly, Armstrong was furious. When the report was discussed at the British Association in 1919 he categorically dismissed it as worthless (which it was not) and as unlikely to influence educational opinion (which it did) (*N.*, 104 (1919), 521–2).

Gregory, who is sometimes portrayed as the enemy of heurism, in fact strongly supported it provided that over-concentration on method was avoided, and that laboratory work was complemented and supplemented by a broad general course of lessons. Nevertheless, it proved to be Gregory's and not Armstrong's, hour (*B.A.R.*, 1919, 354). Training in experimental, scientific method, Gregory recommended, was to be separate from a 'general course of science' based upon descriptive lessons and reading. Supported by Thomson's major recommendation that 'natural science should be included in the general course of education of *all* up to the age of about sixteen', Gregory used the British Association, *Nature* (which he now edited), and the *School Science Review* as platforms to urge the teaching of 'general science' to all children who were unlikely to attend university (D. Thompson, *S.S.R.*, 40 (1958), 109–22). Laboratory work was to be 'different in nature and intention from work that can be regarded as manual training, or from measurements which exemplify purely mathematical principles. It must be used to illustrate subjects dealt with in the classroom – the Science for All' (Gregory, *ibid.*, 1 (1920), 93–4). Meanwhile, on another front, through the influence of scientists like Harold Hartley, physical chemistry, including the ionic theory that Armstrong despised, penetrated the schools and proved an elegant way of using theory to order and unify practical chemistry classes.

Armstrong's disillusionment with these developments, though not with general science *per se*, is best gauged from his essays on the death of Sanderson (below) and on 'Future science of the schools' (*J. Education*, 1925). The trouble, he felt, was the 'implastic' nature of human material. No single system of education could cope with the wide range of social class, sex, age, and ability present in the schools. The utilitarian ideal of the greatest happiness of the greatest number would only come through the development of the kind of a community feeling for science that was practised and preached by Sanderson. Unfortunately, although both Sanderson and he were heretics in the cause of education, Armstrong felt that in his enthusiasm for the 'romance of science' Sanderson had neglected to teach boys scientific method: accuracy and the discipline of thinking effectively, the art of undermining faith rather than creating it through demonstrations. Armstrong's method was 'slow and difficult – too slow for teachers unwilling to take trouble and impatient of results that will count in examinations' (below, 144).

In 1929, F. W. Westaway published his outstanding and influential book, *Science Teaching*. One of his aims was to increase the stock of biology teaching. Whilst he was appreciative of Armstrong's achievements, he was explicit in rejecting heurism. Westaway, who believed heurism too slow and unworkable, suspected that Armstrong had never revealed the true secret of his method, or that he was unaware of its true nature himself. Was it not all sheer personality; 'his rather tart impatience towards his students, his refusal to help them one iota more than is absolutely necessary, his amazingly clever and ever-ready questions to meet the needs of the moment, his resourcefulness under all experimental difficulties, his untiring help to his students, his rather "grumpy manner", and his rare words of praise' (*op. cit.*, 27) that explained his success? The implication was, then, that only teachers with extraordinary personal magnetism could use heurism effectively, and that demonstrations were probably better for class discipline anyway.[33]

Such curt dismissal hurt Armstrong. To him heurism was a practical system that worked. Was it not pedagogically sound and tested by his experiences? His own syllabuses did not have all the faults found by Westaway or the general science followers. He covered subjects broadly and systematically and at the level appropriate to the child. Good teachers could be found or trained, as his experience with the Board Schools showed. Complaints about incompatibility with examinations were invalid; for he would have changed the whole system of examinations anyway. Objections as to cost were exaggerated and were balanced by the need for fewer textbooks. Yet it must be admitted that by 1937 the heuristic method, as originally conceived, had vanished, killed by the examination system, and the collective criticisms of the new psychology, the general science movement, and brilliant writers like Westaway; while as another war and the need for fresh stringent economies closed the 1930s, some teachers again questioned the British emphasis on, or obsession with, laboratory teaching.[34]

But small cells of heuristic teaching continued, notably at Christ's Hospital, where John Bradley began to construct a continuous syllabus of practical problems linked together by the continuity of materials or by the comparison of substances. His philosophically and pedagogically stimulating writings in the *S.S.R.* have been influential in chemistry teaching since Armstrong's death. A true disciple of Armstrong, Bradley's Machian reservations about the status and value of theoretical entities have made him one of the strongest critics of Nuffield Science.[35]

Armstrong first collected his educational writings for

publication by Macmillan in 1903. He saw his *Teaching of Scientific Method* as a critical contribution to the movement to modernise education following the 1902 Education Act. Arranged in non-chronological order, with the constructive essays on heurism and its syllabuses following didactic essays which castigated the educational system, the work's impact was weakened by its lack of co-ordination. Smithells rightly thought it a pity that Armstrong had not distilled his thoughts into a monograph (*N.*, 69 (1904), 289–90). A second edition appeared in 1910 and was reprinted in 1925 when he opened the book with a new prefatory essay reviewing the changes which had taken place a quarter of a century after 'the winter of our discontent'.

Like all pioneers Armstrong tended to overstress and oversell his recommendations. Criticism there was bound to be because he attacked every conceivable area of science education: the curriculum, equipment, teachers, teaching methods, examinations. But the system that was characterised as heurism by critics was frequently remote from Armstrong's intentions; practised only, if at all, by over-enthusiastic, but uninspired, 'disciples'. The effectiveness of heurism was dependent on the teachers; they were the method's weakest point. To convince teachers of the validity of, and need to alter, a method or a curriculum is always a difficult task. Before the beginning of the twentieth century, Armstrong's task was made more difficult because the school system was not geared to understanding, or caring about, the intellectual purpose for which heurism stood. Payment by results, utilitarianism, the class-structure of the variable school system, and the non-flexible codification of elementary education all combined to make change and revolution very difficult.

Armstrong succeeded in achieving significant changes in the educational code, largely by working through the then powerful British Association. From this platform he was able to draw the attention of informed scientists and laymen to the importance of practical work in science teaching. Through the foundation of its Education Section he forged a new, more powerful, weapon for the twentieth century which could unite the public, scientists and science teachers, and, ultimately, the child psychologists. He was also helped by the economic climate and the contemporary pressure from one Royal Commission after another to maintain and improve Britain's industrial position. The faculties which would be developed by practical science would apply to all areas of later life. Industry and national prosperity would benefit from science in the schools. Perhaps we tend to regard such arguments as exaggerated and expedient today when all children meet with science; but Victorian teachers undoubtedly did notice astonishing transformations in children's understanding when they first introduced them to science. It says much for Armstrong's personality, tenacity, and organising ability that by the end of the century he had reshaped British science teaching. However, as heuristic methods took on the nature of routine, child psychology was becoming more scientific; and meanwhile international industrial competition revealed a still serious educational malaise in Great Britain. Criticism of heurism thus became more serious and objective. Yet, whatever the swings of fortune, science teaching in this country has been coloured by Armstrong's viewpoints ever since the 1890s.

Armstrong was a 'character', an individual who was so much the product of a slower age that many of the twentieth-century generation must have found his mannerisms and ideals odd and irrational. His rude 'bedside' manner was usually, however, a deliberately aggressive tactic to disturb scientific or educational complacency. He was an emotional man. His friend F.W. Keeble thought that unlike most well-educated men Armstrong was guided by his feelings, that he made contact with the world by his head and heart (*Obit. Not. Royal Society*, 3 (1940–1), 229). He was interested in everything and everybody: 'in geology, in entomology, in music, pictures, in beautiful scenery, in travel, in teaching, in his old students and their work, in his friends and relations, in young people generally, in controversies, arguments, and much else' (*J.S.C.I.*, 56 (1937), 669). Although too nervous to shine as a lecturer – he over-prepared his material – he was stimulating informally. He liked company, enjoyed committees and meetings. 'He felt it to be his duty to point out in the daily newspapers the errors of governments, departments, universities, and individuals, and to indicate the true path that they ought to take' (*ibid.*). He was in his own milieu a second Dr Johnson, with the same good qualities and faults.

As a scientist he made sound and useful contributions to the development of chemistry, particularly to knowledge of naphthalene derivatives and natural products like the terpenes. To the historian of science his opposition to the ionic theory and his theory of residual affinity are fascinating examples of the ways in which ideas are received and debated by scientific communities.

But it is undoubtedly in the field of education that Armstrong made his most lasting contribution. The '*virus heuristicum Armstrongii*' of discovery methods is no longer something peculiar to Christ's Hospital, but a methodology which is recognised to have its place in infant, junior, and secondary education. How far Armstrong is responsible for the modern use of discovery methods it is difficult to judge; undoubtedly American experiences, which owed nothing to Armstrong, have been influential on modern curricula like the Nuffield schemes, while the

child psychology that he would probably have spurned
has come to support many of his empirical contentions.
Ironically, in the field of tertiary education where he first
forged heurism, teaching methods remain largely didactic
and specialised. Yet it is salutary to see how much of
what he preached is being said today in the different, but
still pioneering, language of 'experience learning', 'child-
centred teaching', 'integrated subjects', 'curriculum development', and discovery methods'. Environmental
studies, project and field work, block time-tabling, were
all either suggested by Armstrong or are logical developments of his ideas.

Trained himself to think and do, he was appalled by the
mental inertia and lack of practical ability of the students
he taught in the 1870s. Within a generation he had pro-
foundly reorganised and influenced methods of scientific
instruction in schools and in the new technical colleges.
Teachers were forced to rethink their textbooks, their own
authoritarian role in the class- or lecture-room, and rediscover the value of training young people to think and
work by themselves. Until the 1960s most school laboratories resembled their ancestral forms at Finsbury Technical College and the Christ's Hospital workshops. No
other nation in the world so emphasises practical teaching in
its schools. Practical science teaching in British schools owed
and owes its success and vitality to Armstrong's heuristic
campaign. In the words of his devoted disciple Charles
Browne, who carried the torch of heurism into the 1940s:

There is probably hardly a teacher of science today whose
methods, consciously or unconsciously, have not been modelled
by Armstrong's crusades. As an original thinker on education,
Armstrong ranks with Huxley; as a constructive reformer he is
pre-eminent ... though years of strife with the conservative
forces of educational tradition may, occasionally, have led us to
policies of expediency, our courage has been maintained by the
faith that he gave us (*Browne*, 24).

Our need to honour Huxley's will
(1933)

When I entered the dominant branch of your school in Oxford Street, sixty-eight years ago – when Biology meant merely Huxley's courses of lectures on Zoology – 'science,' as we are pleased to call it, was only in the making; few to-day can be alive to the primitive conditions under which we then worked. Yet the foundations that had been laid were fundamental and sound. In some directions – in the world of mechanism – the advance is beyond words to picture; in others, our failure to advance, especially to apply scientific method to human control, is all but inexplicable. It is necessarily so, because we have allowed and still allow the men to 'govern' us who have no power of using the method which has led to scientific advance – the bookmen: in a word, because the Oxford spirit still prevails in our administrative system. Words are allowed to count before facts. As an active worker throughout the period, I think I *have* 'seen a great deal'; some account of my experience and the views I have formed may, therefore, not be without value. Here let me say with gratitude how, at last, my ambition is satisfied. I have long waited for such an opportunity as this.

Huxley did not take the opportunity that was his, when I was his pupil, of making me his body slave: if ever man sought to mould himself upon another, however, it is I – having striven, certainly since the early 1880s, to take up the cross he bore in education and as an educational publicist, for cross – with thorns too – it is and ever will be. A master of rhetorical eloquence, he never went far

55

enough to be the bore: I have long since reached that rank – as nothing seems to concern us so little as our children's intellectual health and strength and to talk of it is to bore. Schooling is forced upon us – little use to object – our social apathy to its inefficiencies is appalling – no one seems to see that the present peril of the world is the consequence of our calculated subjection to ignorance. Of course, Huxley tempered education with anti-clericalism and the Church gave him many chances of an occasional hard one with his left: much to public amusement. Today, the clerical Lion complacently thinks that it can lie down comfortably with the 'science' Lamb and that a star-lit peace prevails between them. The Lion does not see how it is caged: how the Lamb now has crossed the bar and out-dares Daedalus, by looking down upon Everest and Kanchenjunga – a mighty achievement! Yet is our culture so low that neither does the Lion roar nor the Lamb even bleat, for instance, at such 'goings-on' with spirits [i.e. Spiritualism] as those of my old friend Sir Oliver Lodge. No man has courage to-day. Huxley would forthwith have put on the gloves in public defence. What he would have said, had he put Sir Oliver's *in futuro* brand of tobacco into his pipe and attempted to smoke it: well, not having known him privately, I cannot say, what would have been the precise line of his 'langwidge.' Strong as is the house that Thomas Henry built for himself, upon the solid chalk, at Eastbourne – it now happens to be in the hands of members of my own family, so I have entry to it and know – my suspicion is, that its stout walls might have fallen, as did those of Jericho before the blast of the trumpets. Had Sir Oliver's brand of celestial whisky also been offered to him, Beachy Head might well have gone down to the sea in the flood. His friend Charles Kingsley's sense of 'sound scientific thought' would certainly have been outraged. Such 'goings-on' stultify all

our ideas of ever making human beings rational by education, even when the training is fortified, between whiles,
by addiction to the stern canons of science . . .

[Huxley's] reputation as a master of education must rest
mainly upon his writings and public addresses, not upon
his work as a teacher. He lectured only to a select class of
students of his subject: putting aside the single course of
illustrative lectures he gave on *Physiography* (1869), he
took no part as a leader in general education work or in
developing method. I owe much to the inspiration and
support of the Herbert Spencer–Huxley school but
mainly 'after the event.' As I hope to show, I fell before
its influence only after much untutored self-preparation.

More than sixty-five years ago, a young beginner, as a
student, in 1866–7, I sat, if not exactly at his feet, in face
of his blackboard and watched him embroider it most
exquisitely with chalks of varied hue: the while he talked
like a book: with absolute precision, in chosen words, so
easily that we were hypnotised by his basilisk artistry into
the absurd belief that we were learning: in fact, we were
just being told, allowed to have no doubts, with no time to
think! He was a marvellous exponent – therefore, a bad
teacher, as are all who are eloquent. This was at the
Schools of Mines in Jermyn Street. The course was purely
formal and descriptive, without living illustration: in those
far-off days, my chosen subject, Chemistry, was the only
one in which laboratory teaching was customary – this we
owed to the great Liebig's foresight. I looked up but was
not fed by Huxley. My young soul shuddered at crayfish
minutiae: it asked for knowledge of life. Since infancy, I
had been an insect lover and hunter: my earliest recollec-
tion is of *Vanessidae* – beautifully dressed Admirals and
Peacocks, wearing every possible decoration in days long

before 'Decorations' were commanded even by the Royal Society, sporting over a wide expanse of stinging nettle in a wild corner of a large garden: the rapture, a few years later of seeing and chasing my first *Clouded Yellow*, on Fairlight Down, remains to the present day an unforgettable vision. I had bred silkworms; kept white mice, rabbits and pigeons; sat long hours, day after day, in quiet thought, angling for roach and dace in the pellucid waters of the Ravensbourne, sprung from a clear Kentish chalk spring, soon to be polluted by an unlovely gas liquor, as are now the roadways and the seas by the foul filth of oil. Some day we shall execrate this, finding the fish gone from the North Sea: the sign up, 'No, Plankton, ye shall not enter here!' I had all sorts of latent interests in the living world and the unconscious desire, innate at puberty, to understand. Those were days before London was a brickyard, when it was surrounded by villages – when the tree was allowed both to exist and to be natural.

In his lectures, Huxley was the letter-perfect exponent of his facts: master of a fine logic but encased in hard bones, never a 'Naturschwärmer.' He confesses to this, in his *Autobiography: 'The only part of my professional course which really and deeply interested me was physiology, which is the mechanical* (sic) *engineering of living machines and notwithstanding that natural science has been my proper business, I am afraid there is very little of the genuine naturalist in me.'*

Fancy regarding physiology as *mechanical engineering*. Huxley knew no chemistry that counted. These are points worth noting, as indications of peculiarities and limitations in our human make-up, to be taken into account in any scheme of education.

On his return from his Australian expedition, he seems to have been overmastered by his craft: he became a severely scientific, comparative morphologist, intensely interested in tracing out affinities – in fact, moulding his mind to appreciate Darwin's evolutionary philosophy. Though highly skilled as a minute anatomist and as a close observer of structure, he was never an experimentalist but essentially a didactic teacher – with a marked tendency to pontificate. Had he been otherwise, more consciously formative and persuasive as a teacher his influence would have been far greater: he would have secured more than a select following of intimates. Men such as H. G. Wells would have been inspired to engage in higher work than mere literary froth-blowing: made closer students of the boundless beauty of Nature, they would not have projected the impossible as our human future and would have preached a higher morality, especially to women.

I would here insist upon the need of drawing a clear distinction between experimental and observational exercises. The inefficiency of our modern school teaching is largely because teachers have not grasped the difference: they have yet to learn how to experiment. They are taught didactically and learn by rote: their 'experiments' are merely verifications or demonstrations in proof of assertions: the *art of discovery* is seldom, if ever, taught either in University or school.

Zoology is a descriptive science and has no *raison d'être* as a separate discipline: form and function are so interdependent, that unless its discipline be closely interwoven with chemistry and physiology, it cannot well be a philosophy or a living science. The fact is, we have learnt that no 'science' can be taught apart. Indeed, when the school was removed to South Kensington (*circa* 1870), seeing the need of practical instruction, Huxley wisely put this side of his subject into commission: into the able hands of Thiselton Dyer, Michael Foster, Ray Lankester and [W.] Rutherford – a more than remarkable crew but with little experience of teaching.

We were then at the beginning of things: you to-day have little idea how primitive the conditions were. A composite subject was in the making. Unfortunately, the crew soon went apart, leaving but a few ribs of an unspecified boat. The Zoology became recitative – little more than a descriptive catalogue in the hands of [G. B.] Howes, Huxley's successor. Botany swarmed off under [F. O.] Bower and gradually lost count of the living plant. Physiology was never developed – Foster carried the infant into the Fens and there acquired great merit as its nurse: the spice of South Kensington infused, through Huxley, into University College blood, in fact, had far-reaching effects, as it made Cambridge what it is to-day. I witnessed the transformation.

A great opportunity was lost of founding a simple, general cultural course of general biology: this has never been regained. Such a course is the crying need of our day, especially at Cambridge. Huxley was not an imaginative, formative teacher, in this particular. He definitely showed lack of generalship. He had the tandem in his grip but lacked constructive outlook; the reins were too long, the team too big, too much for him to hold.

An aside here. Good as was the top floor, it was being beaten, down below in the basement, by the chemist-turned-physicist, [Frederick] Guthrie, who developed a logical, practical course, on self-help lines, of extraordinary value – long since on the scrapheap, I fear; given its final quietus by the all-pervasive electron. It is little short of shameful that South Kensington has let this go by the board – unrecorded. Real earthly physics is a fast-disappearing art. Cannot some-one be found to recover the course, if only to be put away in a case in the British Museum, as a monument of a former greatness? None of Huxley's colleagues, except Guthrie, had the least interest in educational method: no one in the school has had except Abney and he was of the Museum. I ought

*perhaps to mention Perry but he came too late upon the scene
to influence conservative colleagues.*

As to my own development, I have the clearest recol-
lection, that when I became a student of Chemistry at
Oxford Street, my hope was to learn how things had been
found out – that my great desire was to gain knowledge of
method: to find out where all the knowledge came from,
how it had been won. As a lad, I had read omnivorously
and learnt not a little.* With an elder companion I had
feasted upon [*J. H.*] *Pepper's Playbook of Science* [1860] –
in its original form, a far better book than any now available for boys. I had also assimilated [*J. A.*] *Stöckhardt's
Chemistry* [Cambridge, 1850], even gloated over a book by
Berzelius describing laboratory apparatus. I had, however,
the definite feeling that something was wanting: I could
not find any reference to 'origins.' I use the word
advisedly, because the desire to know these came in
through using *Trench's Study of Words*, at school. My
interest in the practice of scientific method, in fact, is of
purely literary origin. The book fascinated me as a lad
and I can now see prevented me from appreciating
Huxley's didactic teaching, perfect though this was. It
made me critical and anxious to get behind meanings:
unfortunately, the unpleasant habit has not only stuck to
me but grown throughout life. Still, in my case, the
Trench seed fell upon prepared ground. I had a critical
father – he was specially critical of words, though I
imagine he had little schooling. He wrote his most important business letters, at home, in the evening; as he
wrote he would often call my attention to words and discuss their fitness: *exploit*, then little used as a verb, was one

---

* As an instance, I may give the unsealing of the King's despatches at
sea, described in Capt. Marryat's *Snarleyow*, by blowing air through
a red-hot dry tobacco-pipe stem upon the wax: a trick I often afterwards used in waxing over corks. (I had a knack of storing such
oddments.)

I always remember; a discussion over *chouse* is another. He was as much interested in Trench as I was. Fortunately, Trench's two books are now in the *Everyman* series – all Huxley's should be, let me say parenthetically.

As a student, under Frankland, I was handling things all the time: really getting to know them; an intuitive understanding of the method of discovery was creeping in. Under Huxley, I was only entertained and I soon ceased to attend his course. I was under no obligation to go to him – my father, knowing nothing of science, throughout my student's career, left me to do as I liked. At most, I took the class examinations; therefore, I am officially unknown by the school. I have ever regretted that I did not attend the Working Men's Lectures Huxley gave, in which he told a consecutive story: they were not supposed to be for young students. His failure to attract me is all the more noteworthy, perhaps, as at the time, week after week, on Saturdays, I was going to St Bartholomew's Hospital, to witness the Surgical operations – in which, for some reason impossible to explain, I took an intense interest, looking on without turning a hair. I made abject apology to Huxley, in later life, by sending two of my sons, on their leaving school, at about seventeen, not as was usual to first year's chemistry and physics courses but directly to the lectures on Biology. I would do so again to-day. There is great need of an open course on physiology for those who have just left school. No school can teach more than the beginnings of real Biology and the need of such teaching is most felt, it is most necessary, at the age when school should be left for some place of higher instruction, under free conditions, away from the school namby-pambyism forced upon our society merely to serve the commercial ends of schools and to relieve teachers of their responsibilities. Unfortunately, your Imperial College has no thought of ordinary public needs: *pace*

Huxley and culture, it only serves commercial ends, to train professionals.

Not only did Huxley fail me. My experience at Jermyn Street, in Geology, under [A. C.] Ramsay, was like that in Zoology. Ramsay lectured at the blackboard and showed only a few rock specimens and unconvincing diagrams. I heard his course through and sat at the examination: years afterwards, I found my marked paper but it meant nothing to me, as I could not recall having heard a word of it. I also tasted the *Mechanics* but soon found the course entirely nauseous. If teaching is to be effective, the horse must be willing to drink: give him full opportunity but use no force – it may be too cold for his stomach at the time. The London University system, which compels passing in every enforced subject, is a sin against nature: a product of the unthinking mind of the bookman.

In fact, I could have learnt Mechanics from Perry.[1] I learnt to use the drawing-board with no other aid than the studies in perspective borrowed from a young friend, a pupil in an architect's office.

The strange variations in the mental rutting period also need to be taken into account. When I was about forty and had children whom I wished to interest in things, I was led to take up geology again but in the field! I was suddenly converted, by a great outburst of *Micraster*[2] over a new face of chalk exposed at Margate, which happened in cutting back the cliff to construct a defensive sea wall. I became a coast walker and section photographer and eventually almost an expert in chalk geology, through association with my deceased friend, Arthur Rowe.[3]

Per contra, attending Tyndall's marvellously illustrated lectures on Physics, also at Jermyn Street, I was enraptured. His Icelandic *Strokur*, spouting up to the ceiling ever lives in my mind's eye. Everything in *Heat as a Mode of Motion*, everything in his *Sound*, was put before us: we really knew what wave motion was. Tyndall's science may have been limp at times – he was no mathematician – but as a teacher he was worth all the Professors of the R.C.S. and R.S.M. put together and no other actor on the Royal Institution stage has ever surpassed him as a popular lecturer. The Cabinet Trick [the ultramicroscope], with which he routed [H.C.] Bastian and other believers in spontaneous generation, is now on show in the R.I. Museum and commands attention to-day as a simple monument to his great experimental genius. It made a profound impression the night of the first performance.

Frankland had no art of oratory but every word told. He was the man of deeds. Starting from Oxford Street, he set an example which made water a safe drink almost the world over. Why is it that, while remembering Huxley, the Imperial College has forgotten the great pioneers of practice on their early staff, his companions Frankland, Tyndall, Guthrie? Only this year we have established, I am glad to say, a Lancastrian Frankland Society,[4] at Lancaster, where he spent his youth, which I hope will aid in making clear the incalculable service he rendered, particularly to public health. Huxley but sought to reform public morals; with little result, if one may judge from writings of his own family; he certainly did not succeed in making education 'safe.'

I was two years and a term at the College. It will be obvious that I managed to crowd a fair amount of tasting into the time – a good deal more than may appear. Being never seen without a book, I was soon made College Librarian and as such devoured everything on its shelves, in English or French; I could not then read German. Frankland imposed upon Horace Brown and myself in proof the whole of his remarkable lecture notes, to test their digestibility. What we could not do in the way of drawing Crum Brown–Frankland Graphic or Glyptic Formulae[5] wasn't worth considering. Notwithstanding all the X-rays say, things mineral to-day look very much as we pictured them, nearly seventy years ago, with the aid of Frankland's too, too utterly simple valency rules. Is no one sufficiently 'Master of this 'ere College' to-day to know what its former Professor of Chemistry did, in laying such foundations, before he became sanitarian? Unfortunately, chemistry is no longer taught as a science nor historically: you have broken up the discipline into five or more unco-ordinated bits, so it comes perhaps that you no longer have the inclination to consider such points of history. Lancaster should shame you into instituting a Frankland as well as a Huxley Lecture: it would have been Huxley's first thought to do justice to his brother (they were members of the X Club). Frankland, be it noted, was a few months Huxley's senior; it is easy for chemists to remember the year of their birth, as it is that in which Benzene was born, in the Royal Institution: three sufficiently notable events to mark a year [1825].

Although so long at the College, I was only a registered student, in systematic training, during a year and a term. In 1867, at the close of the autumn session, Spider Frankland invited the young student Fly to walk into the (private) parlour where Peter Griess and other giants had worked under Hofmann,[6] who was still in office when I entered the College. I was sole occupant of this holy of holies during over a year. The task set me was a revision of the methods of water analysis, mainly with the object of developing an absolute method of determining organic (sewage) impurity. We devised the vacuum combustion process, in which we were the first users, after Graham, of the Sprengel mercury-fall-pump, then a simple single tube. Not until three or four years later did Crookes follow our example and use the pump, in an improved form, in constructing his Radiometer. Meanwhile Frankland and Lockyer were using it, in the spectroscopic work which gave Lockyer his start. We were at the beginning of things. Kekulé gave Benzene its hexagonal garment only in the year in which I entered the Royal College: Benzene Chemistry, Molecular Physics, every sort of modern use of Electricity, are all creations of my epoch.

I was trusted by Frankland to run alone, for the most part. The experience was invaluable and I gained complete self-confidence. Has any student to-day such liberty? Can anyone grow up in his own image? Frankland was one of the three Commissioners appointed in 1868 to inquire into the Pollution of Rivers and the Domestic Water Supply of Great Britain. The work, which lasted six years, put him at the head of the profession.

In the autumn of 1867 I went to Germany, to the University of Leipzig, on Frankland's advice, enlisting under Kolbe, his old companion in arms in Playfair's laboratory, who had enticed him, in early days, to Bunsen's laboratory, in Göttingen [sic, Marburg], where he made his great discovery of Zinc Methyl. I remained two and a half years with Kolbe, only visiting Brunswick – to stay with my student friend, Karl Knapp, Liebig's nephew – and Dresden, the latter on the occasion of the *Naturforscher-Versammlung*: a memorable occasion, as I met Friedel, Crafts, Fittig, Tollens, Ladenburg, Griess and others, afterwards seeing Kekulé, in Bonn, on my way home. I remember Fittig's astonishment at such a stripling being the A of Armstrong and Frankland's *Analysis of Potable Waters*, published the year before (1868) by the Chemical Society. I returned shortly before the Franco–Prussian War of 1870; after taking the Ph.D., by oral examination, in Chemistry with Physics ([W.G.] Hanckel) and Mineralogy ([K.A.] Naumann) as subsidiary subjects. Although these were my selected subjects, I attended the whole of the celebrated [C.F.W.] Ludwig's wonderfully illustrated, vivisectional course on Animal Physiology; also a short special course which we got the anatomist [F.F.] Braun to give on Sunday mornings: the Botany lectures and Praktikum; a course on Agricultural Chemistry by [J.A.] Knop. It should be clear by now that my failure to assimilate Huxley, at Jermyn Street, was not lack of interest in Biology.

University life in Germany, in those days, was simplicity itself and pure delight. We were a happy band of at least a dozen workers, in the Advanced laboratory, all bent upon proving that we could work alone – each with a different problem to solve, each knowing every detail of the other's work. To learn both Chemistry and German, I bought *Liebig's Annalen* and translated paper after paper from its pages, thereby gaining considerable literary – may I say – culture.

On my return, Frankland had nothing to offer but gave me the free run of my old laboratory, where I began to work. At the Chemical Society, I met Williamson, Odling, De la Rue, Abel, Tilden, Groves, Hugo Müller and others. The return of a prodigal son from Germany was then a novelty. Owing to Hofmann being in London and Liebig no longer an attraction, the habit of studying in Germany had ceased, to set in again only gradually, largely owing to enforced emigration, at the instance of the 1851 Commissioners – Lockyer and Roscoe especially.[7] The great mistake the Commissioners made was in not requiring students first to spend a year or so abroad – France as well as Germany should have been visited – and then, on return, at least a year in a home laboratory. We should not then have been in the parlous state of undeveloped efficiency we were in at the outbreak of war, subject to the rule of a lawyer.

After a short interval I was led to join forces with Dr A.

Matthiessen, Lecturer on Chemistry at St Bartholomew's Hospital Medical School. He was one of the early workers on Alkaloids and also a physical chemist, well known for his studies of the electrical conductivities of metals and alloys, as a member of the British Association Electrical Standards Committee. He suggested our working both on Narcotine and on Iron: a fair diversity of subject. He soon transferred to me two special classes on Chemistry, held for students proceeding to the London University Preliminary Scientific and 1st M.B. examinations – having no stomach for such work. I taught these during a dozen years, with no little gain in experience. The work involved coaching pure and simple, as the practical side was only elementary analysis: concentration of attention and organisation of subject were, therefore, called for in no slight measure.

By great good fortune, at the close of 1870 I became Professor of Chemistry at the London Institution, in succession to Wanklyn, who had followed Grove, of battery fame, the first to dissociate water by heated platinum: also the discoverer of the Hydrogen–Oxygen gas battery, cells of which were still in the laboratory, behind the Lecture Theatre. I was thus taken straight into electricity. My chief, Matthiessen, committed suicide in October 1870 and was succeeded by Russell. I have often wondered what would have happened if either Matthiessen had lived on or I had been made his successor: I might have helped to put a little life into medical chemistry. I was now independent, the proud possessor of a laboratory of my own: Professor at an Institution of note – where Huxley had given his course of Lectures on *Physiography* the year before (1869), Carlyle his *Lectures on Heroes*. Smee of battery fame and a pioneer Rock Gardener was a Manager, De la Rue and Daniel Hanbury also were on the Council. The twelve happiest and most fruitful years of my life were those spent at the London Institution, in a laboratory which was little more than a cellar, endeavouring to gain practical mastery of my subject. I was fortunate in having young helpers and we cracked not a few nuts. I had joined the Chemical Society in 1870, was elected on the Council in the spring of 1873 and became one of the Secretaries in 1875, W. H. Perkin, of aniline Dye fame, being my senior colleague. Graebe, the discoverer of the relation of Alizarin to Anthracene and the first to make Alizarin artificially, had been my bench neighbour in the old Leipzig laboratory and had travelled to England in 1869 to meet Perkin, who was his rival as inventor of a process for making Alizarin. In 1876 I was admitted a Fellow of the Royal Society. I also did a large amount of literary work: articles in Watt's *Dictionary of Chemistry*; Chemical Society Abstracts; a primer of Organic Chemistry (1874); a new, almost entirely rewritten, edition of Miller's *Organic Chemistry* (published in 1880); the article on Inorganic Chemistry in the Ninth Edition of the *Encyclopaedia Britannica*. I also marked papers for the Science and Art Department Examinations and for London University.

I finally saw the real light of method, much as I had had inklings of it in the beginning, not through my own subject but through the insight I gained into legal method in the course of a patent action, in the Court of Chancery – a fight over the validity of the patent taken out in protection of Kolbe's method of manufacturing Salicylic Acid from Phenol and Carbon Dioxide. I had learnt to examine and inquire into origins but, up to that time, was not sufficiently alive to the need of a searching cross-examination and judicial consideration of every item of evidence for and against a proposition – the method, I then learnt, which was practised in the Chancery Court.

I thus at last realised that knowledge (Science) was one

thing: the methodical logical use of knowledge (Scientific Method) another; the judicial use something far higher. The essential need of a definite issue was made clear. That Huxley had the judicial mind is obvious, if only from his invention of the word *Agnostic:* he declined to go beyond the facts. He was ever the advocate of the practice of scientific method. None the less, he was eminently didactic and seems to have hugged the belief that method crept in with knowledge – which, in fact, judging from results, it does not. Our modern method is not even to test hypotheses – too often the hypothesis is no sooner propounded than it is accepted as a faith. Our science to-day is for the most part a medley of faiths, if not of religions. We rarely make a distinction between theory and hypothesis, in fact, nearly always prostitute the word theory to the mean sense of speculation.

I now come to the crowning event in my life. A great change and advance in my career came, in October 1879, when the late Professor Ayrton and I entered the service of the then recently established City and Guilds of London Institute for the Advancement of Technical Education. A great responsibility was put upon us. We carried on our work in temporary quarters, until the summer of 1883 when the Finsbury Technical College was opened. Ayrton had gained his experience in the Indian Telegraph service and in Japan, where with others he had been engaged in training the Japanese to use English methods. He had a great opportunity, as we began almost at the moment that electricity came into public use for lighting and power purposes: all the great inventions, beginning with the telephone, came crowding in but even the gas engine was then in a primitive condition and the high-wheel bicycle just coming into vogue. Ayrton's one object was to make his men practical electricians. The method he adopted was much like that followed by Huxley, in the South

Kensington practical course. It was purely didactic. Some of us irreverently termed it the penny-in-the-slot method. The student found himself in face of certain apparatus and the instructions he needed to carry through the verification of this or that theorem – Ohm's law, for example. The method had the great advantage, that the student learnt his lesson by doing instead of being merely told – but with a minimum of effort and little call to think for himself. No element of discovery was involved in the exercise.

My position was entirely different and much more difficult. I had to deal with an age-old subject and put new life into old bones, if possible. I might have had a laboratory to myself – one was planned and the contracts made for its erection, when I was appointed. In like manner, there might have been a special building for electricity; Ayrton would never have been satisfied with less than I had. I, however, had long been alive to the narrow training of the average chemist and was particularly aware of his ignorance of engineering. I at once sought permission to report upon the scheme. The ultimate result was a composite building and the Finsbury course, which made all the first-year subjects common to all students, deferring specialisation, in one or other of three departments, to the second year; this was coupled with an entrance examination to secure the admission of students sufficiently informed to take advantage of the instruction. At no time was there any control by external examinations: we insisted on being entirely free. The subjects chosen were mathematics, engineering drawing and simple workshop practice, chemistry and physics, mainly electricity. Evening classes were also instituted but no combined course in these was arranged. The Central course was established on similar lines but at higher fees. Both Colleges were highly successful and undoubtedly gave a much-needed impetus. The rapid success saved the City Guilds from public inquiry into the administration of their resources.

I had been dissatisfied with the current method of teaching chemistry from the beginning, especially with test-tubing to order: in fact, I had introduced changes even into the simple work for the Preliminary Science and 1st M.B. at St Bartholomew's Hospital. When faced with the task at Finsbury of making my subject appeal not only to chemists but particularly to students of electricity and engineering, mindful of my own early desires and the difficulty of satisfying them, I determined to attempt to lead students to be discoverers from the outset – to train them to use their eyes and to think for themselves, on all possible occasions. The result was the course* made public in 1884, in the Educational Section of the Health Exhibition, partly held in the new Central Technical College building. In principle, the course remained in operation until 1912, when our system was wickedly destroyed by Sir William White's jealous and incompetent interference. I simply developed the age-old method of the infant and the detective, in place of didactic teaching. I taught very little chemistry but a great deal of chemical method. Since then, your engineering students have no longer been taught the chemistry that is good for engineers, assimilable by their simple intellects: instead, they have been doped with the chemistry that is bad even for chemists. You have omitted drawing from your entrance examination and it is no longer in any way compulsory for chemists to take engineering; the soul is gone out of the course. My system was necessarily historical: the study of combustion phenomena and of limestone came first. Black, Cavendish, Lavoisier, Priestley, Scheele were the

* Described in *The Teaching of Scientific Method*, 1st ed., 1903. Macmillan & Co. [below, p. 74]

prototypes. Alcohol was brought in early to usher in structural chemistry. The essence of the system lay in first posing a question or problem – in fact, in stating the crime to be unravelled. Conjoined with this was the obligation to write down, as a coherent story, *there and then*, as the inquiry went on, in direct, descriptive language, readable and judicial, whatever was thought and done, whatever conclusions were deduced. The greatest nonsense is talked about the impossibility of making the student discover everything for himself – no one asks that he should or believes that he can: only that he shall learn how discoveries are made, first by children, then by ordinary detectives, then by discoverers proper. Always something noteworthy is first observed – then the chase begins. A few scientific Edgar Wallaces might galvanise the public into finding out something about themselves and their surroundings. Apparently, teachers in schools, with rare exceptions, never will: they have no imagination, having never found out anything by themselves or learnt to dream.

After thirty-five years' closest experimental study of the problem, I am satisfied that, from Huxley onwards, we have all been to sanguine in the expectation that 'scientific education' can be made palatable to the many. We have vastly over-rated the possibilities and the value of education, in every field: few are really educable to any extent.

A Huxley Memorial Lecture at Imperial College of Science and Technology on 4 May 1933. Printed as a pamphlet, London, 1933.

*On the teaching of Natural Science as a part of
the Ordinary School Course and on the method
of teaching Chemistry in the Introductory
Courses in Science Classes, Schools and Colleges*
(1884)

However fully it may be admitted by the few that it is
important, nay essential, that all members of the community, whatever their station or occupation, should
receive some instruction in the elements of Natural
Science during their school career, the general public have
not as yet had brought home to them with sufficient
clearness that just as a knowledge of foreign languages is
essential to all who are brought into intercourse with
foreigners, so in like manner is a correct knowledge of the
elements of natural science of direct practical value to all
in their daily intercourse with Nature, apart from the
pleasure which such knowledge affords. In fact, judged
from a purely utilitarian standpoint, the advantages to be
derived from even the most elementary acquaintance with
what may be termed the science of daily life are so mani-
fold that if once understood by the public, the claims of
science to a place in the ordinary school course must meet
with universal recognition. To quote Huxley: 'Knowledge of Nature is the guide of practical conduct . . . any
one who tries to live upon the face of this earth without
attention to the laws of Nature will live there for but a very
short time, most of which will be passed in exceeding dis-
comfort: a peculiarity of natural laws, as distinguished
from those of human enactment, being that they take effect
without summons or prosecution. In fact, nobody could
live for half a day unless he attended to some of the laws of
Nature; and thousands of us are dying daily or living

miserably, because men have not yet been sufficiently zealous to learn the code of Nature.'

But it is also and mainly on other and far higher grounds that we should advocate universal practical teaching of the elements of natural and more particularly of so-called physical science: viz. that it tends to develop a side of the human intellect which, I believe, I am justified in saying is left uncultivated even after the most careful mathematical and literary training: the faculty of observing and of reasoning from observation and experiment. It is entirely from this latter point of view that I shall venture to propound a scheme for teaching the elements of that branch of physical science with which I am most intimately acquainted . . .

The great objection to the method at present in vogue appears to me to be that it is practically the same whether science is taught as a part of the general school course or whether it is taught professionally: in other words, a lad studies chemistry, for example, at school in just the same way as at a science college, the only difference being that he does not carry his studies so far at school as at college. This, I believe, is the primary fault in our present system. In my opinion, no single branch of natural science should be selected to be taught as part of the ordinary school course but the instruction should comprise the elements of what I have already spoken of as the science of daily life and should include astronomy, botany, chemistry, geology, mechanics, physics, physiology and zoology – the olla podrida comprehended by Huxley under physiography but which is perhaps more happily expressed in the German word *Naturkunde* – in so far as is essential to the understanding of the ordinary operations and objects of Nature, the teaching from beginning to end being of as practical a character as possible and of such a kind as to cultivate the intelligence and develop the faculties of observing, comparing and reasoning from observation; and the more technical the course the better. The order in which these subjects should be introduced is matter for discussion; personally, I should prefer to begin with botany and to introduce as soon as possible the various branches of science in no particular order but that best suited to the understanding of the various objects or phenomena to which the teaching for the time being had reference. The extent to which instruction of this kind is given must entirely depend on the class of scholars.

There are few teachers capable of giving such instruction and fewer books of a character suited to ordinary requirements. The development of such a system will, in fact, require the earnest co-operation of a number of specialists; but apart from the difficulty of securing efficient co-operation, there is no reason why some such scheme should not be elaborated at no distant date. If action is to be taken, however, there must be no delay or the opportunity will be lost. I trust that this meeting will be prepared to give much attention to this question and that it may be possible to continue the discussion on other platforms, as it is fundamentally important and deserving of the most serious consideration of educationalists. No doubt it will be said that the object of introducing the teaching of science into the school course is to afford mental training of a particular character, not the inculcation of useful knowledge, and that this end can be secured by teaching well some one branch of science. Admitting that this has been the case, however, there is no reason why it should be in the future: if while developing the intellect it be possible – and it certainly is – to impart much valuable information; and if – as it certainly is – the teaching be rendered easier and more attractive because it has direct reference to the familiar objects and operations of Nature. We cannot, indeed, any longer afford to grow up ignorant of all that is going on around us and without learning to use our eyes and our reasoning powers; we cannot afford to be un-acquainted with the fundamental laws of health; but we must ever remember 'that knowledge of Nature is the guide of practical conduct' and no effort must be spared to render our system of education an effectual preparation and truly adapted to the exigencies of practical life. The female educators appear already to have grasped the im-portance of such teaching and under the guise of domestic economy much that I advocate is being taught in girls' schools; it is to be hoped that ere long something akin to the domestic economy course in girls' schools will find a place in boys' schools.

To pass now to the consideration of the mode of teach-ing my own special subject in science classes such as those held under the auspices of the Science and Art Department and in the introductory course for students in science schools and colleges generally. To deal first with the former. Inspection of the syllabus for the elementary stage, together with the study of the examination papers of the past few years, will show that the student is mainly required to have an elementary knowledge of the methods of preparing and also of the properties of the commoner *non-metallic* elements and their chief compounds. There is thus practically no distinction to be drawn between the knowledge required of students under the Science and Art Department and of those who are making the study of chemistry the business of their lives. But surely it is not the function of the Science and Art Department to train up chemists and I am satisfied that it is neither their desire nor their intention to do so; their object undoubtedly is to encourage the teaching of chemistry as a means of culti-vating certain faculties and in order that the fundamental laws of chemistry may be understood and their commoner applications realised. It is not difficult to understand how the system has grown up and why it is maintained; I do not believe it is because the Department consider it a satisfactory one: it is because they know full well that a better system is not yet developed and that it would be unwise to legislate far in advance of the intelligence and powers of the majority of the teachers. With all deference, however, I venture to add that the programme has been drawn up too much from the point of view of the specialist and that too little attention has been devoted to it from the point of view of the educationalist. The course I am inclined to advocate would be of a more directly useful character. There is no reason why in the beginning attention should be confined to the non-metals, especially when certain of the metals enter so largely into daily use; and provided that it involve no sacrifice of the opportunities of developing the faculties which it is our special object to cultivate by the study of chemistry, there is no reason against but every reason for, selecting subjects of everyday importance rather than such as are altogether outside our ordinary experience, such, for example, as the oxides of nitrogen: even chlorine, except in relation to common salt, might be omitted from special study. The presumed distinction between so-called inorganic and organic chemistry should be altogether put aside and forgotten and the elements of the chemistry of the carbon compounds introduced at a very early stage in order that the phenomena of animal and plant life might come under consideration. To give the barest possible outline of a programme, I would include such subjects as the following in the syllabus:

The chemistry of air, of water and of combustion. The distinction between elements and compounds. The fundamental laws which regulate the formation of compounds and the chemical action of bodies upon one another (i.e. the nature of so-called chemical change). The chemical properties of the metals in ordinary use with special references to their uses and the action upon them of air, water, etc. The composition of natural waters. The distinction between fats, carbohydrates and albuminous [protein] substances in so far as is essential to the understanding of the relative values of different foods and respiration and growth in animals and plants (outlines of the chemistry of animal and plant life, in fact); the nature of the processes of fermentation, putrefaction and decay.

The instruction in these subjects should in all cases be imparted by means of object lessons and tutorial classes; lectures pure and simple should, as far as possible, be avoided. The students should by themselves go through a number of practical exercises on the various subjects. I would abolish the teaching of [qualitative analysis] tables for the detection of simple salts, the teaching of analysis, as at present conducted, being, I believe, in most cases, of very little if any use except as enabling teachers to earn grants.

In schools and colleges in which chemistry is taught as a science, ostensibly with the object of training young people to be chemists, it is the almost invariable practice that the student first devotes more or less time to the preparation of the commoner gases and then proceeds to study qualitative analysis; quantitative determinations are made only during the later period of the course. I believe that the system has two great faults: it is too mechanical and it does not sufficiently develop the faculty of reasoning from observation; moreover actual practice in measurement is introduced far too late in the course. It is of great importance that the meaning of the terms equivalent, atomic weight, molecular weight should be thoroughly grasped at an early stage: according to my experience this is very rarely the case; no difficulty is met with, however, if the beginner be taught to make a few determinations himself of equivalents, etc., as he very well may be. It is not necessary here to enter into a more detailed criticism but I propose instead to give a brief description of a modification of the existing system which in my hands, in the course of about four years' experience, has furnished most encouraging results and which I venture to think is worthy of an extended trial.

Instead of merely preparing a variety of gases, the student is required to solve a number of problems experimentally: to determine, for example, the composition of air and of water; and the idea of measurement is introduced from the very beginning as the determination is made quantitatively as well as qualitatively. Each student receives a paper of instructions – two of which are printed as an appendix to this paper – which are advisedly made as bare as possible so as to lead him to find out for himself or inquire how to set to work; he is particularly directed that, having made an experiment, he is to enter in his notebook an account of what he has done and of the result; and he is then and there to ask himself what bearing the result has upon the particular problem under consideration: having done so, he is to write down his conclusion. He is thus at once led to consider what each experiment teaches: in other words, to reason from observation. Apart from the mental exercise which this system affords, if the writing out of the notes be properly supervised, the literary exercise which it also affords is of no mean value.

In illustration, I may here very briefly describe the manner of working out the second problem in the course. The problem being: To determine the composition of water, the student receives the instruction:

1. Pass steam over red-hot iron brads, collect the escaping gas and apply a light to it. (N.B. The gas thus produced is called hydrogen.) He is provided with a very simple apparatus, consisting of a small glass flask containing

water, joined by a narrow bent glass tube to an iron tube (about 9 inches long and $\frac{1}{2}$ to $\frac{3}{4}$ inch wide) in which the brads are placed, a long glass tube suitably bent for the delivery of the gas being attached to the other end of the iron tube. Plaster of Paris is used instead of corks to make the connexions with the iron tube. The iron tube is supported over a burner and heated to redness; the water in the flask is then heated to boiling and the steam thus generated is passed over the brads; the escaping gas is collected over water in the usual manner. Having made this experiment and observed that on passing steam over red-hot iron the gas hydrogen is produced, the student proceeds to consider the bearing of this observation. The hydrogen must obviously be derived either from the water or from the iron, if not from both. Those who already know that iron is iron, so to speak, at once infer that the hydrogen is derived from the water: it is, however, pointed out that, even if it be known that iron is a simple substance, this observation taken alone does not prove that hydrogen is contained in water.

2. The student next learns to prepare hydrogen by the ordinary method of dissolving zinc in diluted sulphuric acid and makes a few simple experiments whereby he becomes acquainted with the chief properties of the gas.

3. Having done this, he is instructed 'to burn dry hydrogen at a glass jet underneath a cold surface and to collect and examine the product'. The product is easily recognised as water. The immediate answer to the question 'What does this observation teach?' is, that since iron is absent, taken in conjunction with experiment 1, the production of water on burning hydrogen in air, the composition of which has already been determined, is an absolute demonstration that hydrogen is contained in water.

4. Having previously studied the combustion of copper, iron and phosphorus in air and having learnt that

when these substances burn they enter into combination with the oxygen in air, the student is also led to infer from the observation that hydrogen burns in air, producing water, that most probably it combines with the oxygen and that water contains oxygen besides hydrogen. It may be, however, it is then pointed out, that the hydrogen, unlike the phosphorus, etc., combines with the nitrogen instead of with the oxygen or perhaps with both. He is, therefore, instructed to pass oxygen over heated copper, weighing the tube before and after the operation; and to heat the 'oxide of copper' subsequently in a current of hydrogen. He then observes that water is formed, the oxygen being removed from the copper: and since nitrogen is absent, it follows that water consists of hydrogen and oxygen and of these alone.

5. By repeating this last experiment so as to ascertain the loss in weight of the copper oxide tube and the weight of water produced, the data are obtained for calculating the proportions in which hydrogen and oxygen are associated in water.

In practice, the only serious difficulty met with has been to induce students to give themselves the trouble to consider what information is gained from a particular observation; to be properly inquisitive, in fact. I cannot think that this arises, as a rule, from mental incapacity. When we consider how the child is always putting questions and that nothing is more beautifully characteristic of young children than the desire to know the why and wherefore of everything they see, I fear there can be little doubt that it is one of the main results – and it is indeed a lamentable result – of our present school system that the natural spirit of inquiry, inherent to a greater or less extent in every member of the community, should be thus stunted in its growth instead of being carefully developed and properly directed.

Having studied, in the manner which I have described, air, water, the gas given off on heating common salt with sulphuric acid and the ordinary phenomena of combustion, the student next receives a paper with directions for the comparative study of lead and silver (see Appendix). The experiments are chosen so as to afford an insight into the principles of the methods ordinarily employed in qualitative and quantitative analyses. The student who has conscientiously performed all the exercises is in a position to specialise his studies in whatever direction may be desirable.

The system I have thus advocated undoubtedly involves far more trouble to the teacher than that ordinarily followed; but the student learns far more under it and I assert with confidence that the training is of a far higher order and also of a more directly useful character. I believe it to be generally applicable and that it would be of special advantage in those cases in which only a short time can be devoted to the study of chemistry – as in evening classes and medical schools. At present the only practical teaching vouchsafed to the majority of students in our large medical schools is a short summer course during which they are taught the use of certain analytical tables: as a mental exercise, the training they receive is of doubtful value; the knowledge gained is of little use in after life; and the course certainly ought not to be dignified by being spoken of as a course of Practical Chemistry: *test-tubing* is the proper appellation. It is not a little remarkable also that even the London University Syllabus nowhere specifies that a knowledge even of the elements of quantitative analysis will be required of candidates either at the Preliminary Scientific or First M.B. Examination and this too when, as is well known, an analysis to be of any practical value must almost invariably be quantitative. It is little less than a disgrace to the medical profession that a subject of such vital importance as chemistry should be so neglected.

If, however, we are to make any change in our method of teaching science, if we are to teach science usefully throughout the country, two things are necessary: teachers of science must take counsel together and the examining boards must seriously consider their position. There can be little doubt that in too many cases the examinations are suited to professional instead of to educational requirements; and that the professional examinations are often of too general a character and do not sufficiently take into account special requirements.

APPENDIX

PROBLEM: TO DETERMINE THE COMPOSITION OF AIR

N.B. – Immediately after performing each experiment indicated in this and subsequent papers, write down carefully a description of the manner in which the experiment has been done, of your observations and the result or results obtained and of the bearing of your observations and the result or results obtained on the problem which you are engaged in solving. Be especially on your guard against drawing conclusions which are not justified by the result of the experiment; but, on the other hand, endeavour to extract as much information as possible from the experiment.

1. Burn a piece of *dry* phosphorus in a confined volume of air, i.e. in a stout Florence flask closed by a caoutchouc stopper. Afterwards withdraw the stopper under water, again insert it when water ceases to enter and measure the amount of water sucked in. Afterwards determine the capacity of the flask by filling it with water and measuring this water.

N.B. – The first part of the experiment requires care and must be done under direction.

2. Allow a stick of phosphorus lashed to a piece of stout wire to remain for some hours in contact with a known volume of air

confined over water in a graduated cylinder. After noting the volume of the residual gas, introduce a burning taper or wooden splinter into it.

N.B. – The residual gas is called *nitrogen.*

3. Burn a piece of dry phosphorus in a current of air in a tube loosely packed with asbestos. Weigh the tube, etc., before and after the experiment.

4. Repeat Experiment 2 with iron-borings moistened with ammonium chloride solution. Preserve the residual gas.

5. Suspend a magnet from one arm of a balance; having dipped it into finely divided iron, place weights in the opposite pan; when the balance is in equilibrium, set fire to the iron.

6. Pass a current of dry air through a moderately heated tube containing copper. Weigh the tube before and after the experiment; also note the alteration in the appearance of the copper.

7. Strongly heat in a *dry* test-tube the red substance obtained by heating mercury in contact with air. At intervals plunge a glowing splinter of wood into the tube. Afterwards note the appearance of the sides of the tube. (Before performing this experiment ask for directions.)

N.B. – The gas obtained in this experiment is named *oxygen.*

8. Heat a mixture of manganese dioxide and potassium chlorate in a dry test-tube; at intervals plunge a glowing splinter into the tube. This experiment is to acquaint you with an easy method of preparing oxygen in quantity.

9. Prepare oxygen as in Experiment 8 and add it to the nitrogen from Experiment 4 in sufficient quantity to make up the bulk to that of the air taken for the latter experiment. Test the mixture with a burning taper or splinter.

10. Dissolve copper in nitric acid and collect the escaping gas (nitric oxide); add some of it to oxygen and some of it to air.

11. Fill a large flask provided with a well-fitting caoutchouc stopper and delivery tube with ordinary tap water and gradually heat the water to the boiling point; collect the gas which is given off in a small cylinder and add nitric oxide to it. Also collect a sufficient quantity in a narrow graduated cylinder and treat it as in Experiment 2.

COMPARATIVE STUDY OF SILVER AND LEAD

SILVER. – *Symbol,* Ag (*Argentum*) *Atomic weight,* 107·67. *Specific heat,* 0·05701.

LEAD. – *Symbol,* Pb (*Plumbum*). *Atomic weight,* 206·47. *Specific heat,* 0·03140.

1. Determine the relative density of lead and silver at a known temperature by weighing in air and in water.

2. Separately heat known weights of lead and silver for some time in the air, allow to cool, then weigh.

3. Separately convert known weights of lead and silver into nitrates; weigh the latter. From the data thus obtained calculate the *equivalents* of lead and silver.

4. Convert the known weights of nitrates thus obtained into chlorides; weigh the latter.

5. Compare the action on lead and silver of chlorhydric [hydrochloric] acid; of dilute and concentrated sulphuric acid, using the acid both cold and hot; and of cold and hot nitric acid.

6. Using solutions of the nitrates, compare their behaviour with chlorhydric and sulphuric acids, hydrogen sulphide, potassium iodide and potassium chromate. Ascertain the behaviour of the precipitate formed by chlorhydric acid when boiled with water and when treated with ammonia solution.

7. Compare the behaviour of lead and silver compounds on charcoal before the blow-pipe.

8. Tabulate the results of your experiments with lead and silver in parallel columns.

9. Ascertain whether the substances given you contain lead or silver.

10. Determine silver in an alloy of lead and silver by cupellation.

11. Study the method of determining silver volumetrically by means of a *standard solution* of ammonium thiocyanate. Determine the percentage of silver in English silver coinage.

12. Determine silver as chloride by precipitation.

13. Dissolve a known weight of lead in nitric acid, precipitate it as sulphate, collect and weigh the latter.

14. What are the chief ores of lead and silver? How are lead and silver extracted from their ores? How is silver separated from lead? How is it separated from burnt Spanish pyrites?

What are the chief properties and uses of lead and of silver?
State the composition of the chief alloys of lead and silver.

. . . .

In reply to the discussion [*not reproduced*]
Professor Armstrong said that it was a source of great
gratification to him, that some of the points which he had
submitted for discussion had been so well taken up. He
thought that this augured well for the future. With regard
to the Science and Art Department, he hoped that it
would be fully understood that what had been said by him
had been in no way said in the form of complaint. He
believed that the Department had done a very great work
indeed in this country, and that they could not too highly
appreciate the services of those who had been at the bottom
of the science teaching. All that he had done had been to
criticise, from the outside point of view, the present requirements of the Department, and to indicate the nature
of the change which it was desirable for them to make as
soon as they found that the ground was fit for them. He
was sure that they were only waiting for that. As he had
already said, he did not believe for a moment that they
were satisfied with their system; but at present they could
not make much alteration. The very great difficulty that
teachers were in at the present time, with regard to the
introduction of any new departure in their system of
teaching, arose from the influence exercised by the various
examining boards; and the only way in which that
influence could be modified was, of course, by discussions
of this kind. As soon as it was known that teachers were
adopting more rational methods, the examinations would
probably be altered in accordance with them. He had
been connected with the examinations of the Science and
Art Department for the last ten years, and he had known
the results of more than a hundred thousand papers; and
he was sure that, whatever the requirements of the

Department had been, the good teachers had always met with very fair reward under that system. In many cases, no doubt, the material at the disposal of the teachers had been very bad, and even good teachers had been unlucky on that account. Of course the nature of the material must be taken into consideration; but those teachers who had had fair average material at their disposal had, in the long run, got their deserts. What was more particularly wanted at the present time was some system of examination more elastic than the present one, and which would enable the examiners to test the knowledge of students and find out when they were crammed and when they really knew their subject. That was the great difficulty in the present system of written examinations. It was perfectly impossible now to find out whether a man had only studied the subject for a few weeks, or whether he had properly studied it. The introduction of such a system as he had proposed would render that result impossible. He did not propose to put this system in the place of lectures. He merely proposed to supplement the lectures by means of this system . . . In giving an introductory course, he usually adopted [this] plan. He generally found that the result of attending a lecture was very poor indeed, and that the ideas obtained by the students were very vague. It was only when they came to repeat the experiments for themselves that they really got a proper idea of the subject. There was no difficulty in working a comparatively large class upon the plan which he had advocated. It would certainly require more individual attention on the part of the teacher, because the great feature of the system consisted in revising the notebooks, in order to see that the experiments had produced the proper result. The great difficulty of the method lay in this work of revision. The difficulty of taking notes might be got over by the lecturer giving out at the beginning of the lecture a series of questions and making the lecture an answer to those questions. That method operated very well with the better class of students, and they gradually got into the habit of taking good notes.

. . .

Reprinted from *International Conference on Education Proceedings* (London, 1884), vol. II, pp. 69–82 and 104–6. The essay, without the discussion, also appeared in *Chemical News*, 50(1884), 239–42, and all editions of Armstrong's *Scientific Method*.

*Suggestions for a course of elementary instruction
in Physical Science*
(1889)

Although the Committee is ostensibly charged to report
as to methods of teaching *chemistry*, chemistry pure and
simple is not what is generally required in schools: therefore the Committee must be prepared to take into consideration and make recommendations for a course of
instruction, preliminary to the natural science course
proper, which in their opinion affords the most suitable
and efficient preparation for later natural science studies.

After the most careful consideration of the question
during at least ten years past; after long holding the
opinion that chemistry as usually understood is not the
most suitable science subject for school purposes: I am
now of opinion that a course which is mainly chemical is
not only the best but also the only one possible if we are to
secure all the objects aimed at in introducing science teaching into schools. Those objects are essentially: to train
boys and girls to use their brains; to train their intelligence; to make them observing and reasoning beings,
accurate observers and accurate thinkers; to teach them to
experiment – and that, too, always with an object – more
frequently than not with what may be termed a logical
object – not for mere descriptive purposes; to inculcate
gradually the power of 'doing,' on which Charles Kingsley
has laid so much stress and which undoubtedly is the
main factor of success in life. It can scarcely be gainsaid
that, through chemistry more than through any other
branch of natural science, it is possible to give precisely
that kind of 'practical' training so requisite at the present
day, because the student is able to ascertain *by experiment*

what are the exact facts and thus arrive independently at an explanation, whereas in the case of other sciences, more often than not, the explanation of necessity, has to be given by the teacher.

Chemistry as usually taught loses greatly in educational value because pupils are told, more often than not, that 'such and such *is* the case,' instead of being taught *how it has been found out* that such is the case; indeed, that which has to be proved is usually taken for granted. Practical chemistry, as a rule, hitherto has been interpreted to mean the preparation of a few gases, etc., and the analysis of simple salts. Much useful information may be and is occasionally imparted during the performance of exercises of this kind but the tendency undoubtedly is for analysis to degenerate into a mechanical drill; and looking at the question from the practical point of view and considering what is the general outcome of such teaching, probably we are bound to agree that the results thus far obtained are usually unsatisfactory. The difficulty, however, is to devise a course sufficiently simple in conception the cost of which is not too great when it is carried into practice; but with respect to this item of cost the Committee has to make clear to parents and teachers the claim of natural science to a fair and proportionate share of the total expenditure, which certainly has never yet been granted to it. By the introduction of such studies into the school course, a set of faculties are trained which it is all-important to develop but which hitherto have been allowed to remain dormant, if not to atrophy, through neglect – which, as all competent authorities admit, cannot possibly be developed by any amount of attention to literary and mathematical studies. It is often not sufficiently clearly stated or understood that the advocates of natural science studies have no desire to displace any of the traditional subjects from the school course; that all that they ask for is a fair share of the child's time, attention and brains – a share proportionate to the effect which such studies can demonstrably produce in developing the mental faculties of the individual: that, in fact, natural science claims to co-operate and in no sense puts in an appearance as a rival.

STAGE I – *Lessons on Common and Familiar Objects*

The first stage of instruction must be one of simple object lessons but these should have an intimate relation to the child's surroundings and should be made the pegs on which to hang many a tale. Probably the most satisfactory and practical mode of commencing is to get children to draw up lists of familiar and common objects under various heads, such as

Natural objects.

Things used in building construction.

Things from which household furniture is made or which are in daily use.

Things used as clothing.

Food materials.

The children should be induced to describe these from observation, as far as possible; to classify them according to their origin into mineral and animal and vegetable or organic; and occasion should be taken at this stage to give by means of reading lessons and demonstrations as much information as possible about the different things, their origin, how made and their uses. It is obvious that in this way a great deal of geography and natural history (*Naturkunde*) might be taught in an attractive manner. Geikie's *Science Primer on Physical Geography* [1872] is the type of book which may be worked through with great advantage at this stage.

STAGE II – *Lessons in Measurement*

This stage should be entered upon as soon as children have learnt the simple rules of arithmetic and are able to add, subtract, multiply and divide – and to use decimals.

Lineal measurements may be first made, using both an English footrule with the inch subdivided in various ways and a metric rule subdivided into millimetres. In this way the relation of the two scales is soon learnt insensibly.

Measurements of rectangular figures and the calculation of their areas may then be made.

After this the use of the balance may be taught and the relation between the English and French systems may be learnt by weighing the same objects with the two kinds of weights. Use may then be made of the balance in determining the areas of irregular figures by cutting out rectangular and irregular figures from the same cardboard or thin sheet metal and weighing these, etc.

Solid figures are next studied: a number of cubes made from the same wood having been measured, their volumes are then calculated and the results thus obtained are compared with those which are obtained on weighing the cubes. The dimensions and weights of cubes made from different woods or other materials are then ascertained and thus it is observed that different materials differ in *density*. The study of the *relative density* of things generally is then entered upon. The ordinary method is easily learnt and used by children, a suitable bottle being provided by filing a nick down the stopper of a common two-ounce narrow-mouth bottle; it may then be shown that the same results are obtained by the hydrostatic method of weighing in air and water and it is not difficult to lead children to understand this latter method after they have determined the heights of balancing columns of liquids such as turpentine, water and saturated brine, of which they have previously ascertained the relative density. These hydro-static experiments are of value at a later stage in considering the effects of atmospheric pressure.

By determining the dimensions of a cube and the weight of the water which it will displace, an opportunity is afforded to point out that if the results are expressed in cubic centimetres and grams respectively, there is a prac-tical agreement between the numbers; it is then easy to explain the origin of the metric system of weights and the relationship between its measures and weights; the irrationality of the English system may also be pointed out.

The relative densities of a large number of common substances having been ascertained, the results may be tabulated and then the value of the data as criteria may be insisted on; as an illustration of their value, quartz, flint, sand and gravel pebbles may be selected: the children having determined their relative densities, the agreement between the results may be pointed out and the identity of the material explained. By drawing perpendiculars corresponding in height to the densities of various sub-stances, a graphic representation is obtained which serves to bring out the value of the graphic method of representa-tion.

A very valuable exercise to introduce at this stage is based on the well-known fact that in certain conditions of the atmosphere things appear moist: a muslin bag full of seaweed may be hung up under cover but freely exposed and may then be weighed daily at a given time; simultan-eously the state of the weather, direction of the wind, the height of the barometer and the state of the wet and dry bulb theromometer may be noted; on tabulating the re-sults, especially if the graphic method be adopted, the variations and their relationship will be noticeable.

Familiarity with the thermometer having been thus

gained, this instrument may be used to examine melting ice and boiling water; the construction of both the Centigrade and Fahrenheit thermometers may then be explained and the effect of heat on bodies made clear. The density of ice and of water at various temperatures may then be determined, a Sprengel tube[8] – which is easily made – being used for warm water; the bursting of pipes in winter, the formation of ice on the surface of water, etc., may then be explained. Afterwards, simple determinations of the heat capacity of a few metals, etc. and of the latent heat of water and steam may be made in accordance with the directions given in a book such as Worthington's *Practical Physics*.

STAGE III – *Studies of the Effect of Heat on things in general; of their behaviour when burnt*

As it is a matter of common observation that heat alters most things, the effect of heating things in general should be studied; in the first instance qualitatively but as early as possible afterwards, also quantitatively. Bits of the common metals may be heated in the bowl of an ordinary clay pipe plunged into a clear place in any ordinary fire or in such a pipe or a small iron spoon over a gas flame. The difference in fusibility is at once apparent. In the case of metals like iron and copper it is noticeable that although fusion does not take place, a superficial change is produced; the gradual formation of a skin on the surface of fused lead and tin is also easily perceived. Observations like this become of great importance at a later stage and indeed serve to suggest further experiments: this is a point of special importance. From the beginning of this stage great attention should be paid to inculcating habits of correct observation; the effect should first be recorded by the pupil, the notes should then be discussed and their incompleteness pointed out and they should afterwards be rewritten. The fusibility of substances which are not affected when heated in the tobacco-pipe may be tested by heating them with a Fletcher gas blow-pipe on charcoal; and by heating little bits of wire or foil in such a flame it is easy for children to discover the changes which metals undergo when burnt, especially in cases such as that of zinc or copper or iron.

The further study of the effect of heat should be quantitative and may well commence with water. It being observed that water disappears on heating, water may be put into a clock glass or glass dish placed on a water-bath (small saucepan); it evaporates and it is then observed that something is left. A known quantity of water by weight or volume is therefore evaporated and the residue weighed. This leads to the discovery that water contains something in solution. The question then naturally arises, What about the water that escapes? so the steam is condensed and the distilled water evaporated. The conception of pure water is thus acquired. An experiment or two on dissolution – using salt and sugar – may then be introduced, a water-oven or even an air-oven (a small Fletcher oven[9]) kept at a known temperature being used and the residue dried until the weight is constant. Rain- and sea-water may next be examined; the results afford an opportunity of explaining the origin of rain and of accounting for the presence of such a large quantity of dissolved matter in sea-water. Then the various common food materials may be systematically studied, commencing with milk; they should first be dried in the oven, then carbonised and the amount of char determined, then burnt and the percentage of ashes determined. A small platinum dish, 15 to 20 grams in weight, is required for these experiments; a gas muffle furnace is of the greatest use in burning the char and in oxidising metals. In addition to the discipline afforded by such experiments, a large amount of valuable information is acquired and the all-important fact is established that food materials generally are combustible substances. Afterwards mineral substances are examined in a similar manner, such as sand, clay, chalk, sulphur, etc.; then metals such as lead, copper, tin and iron may be studied; the increase in the weight of these latter is in striking contrast to the inalterability of substances like sand and salt and the destruction of vegetable and animal substances. Chalk, from which lime is made by burning, is found to occupy a middle position, losing somewhat in weight when strongly heated. The exceptional behaviour of coal among mineral substances and of salt among food materials, is shown to be capable of explanation inasmuch as coal is in reality a vegetable and salt a mineral substance; but sulphur remains an instance of exceptional behaviour requiring explanation. It is not exceptional in being combustible – as metals like magnesium and zinc are combustible – but in affording no visible product. The smell of burning sulphur, however, serves to suggest that perhaps after all there is a something formed which is an invisible substance, possessed of an odour and then follows quite naturally the suggestion that perhaps in other cases where no visible or perceptible product is obtained – as on burning charcoal, for instance – there may nevertheless be a product. Whereas, therefore, in Stage I the pupil will have learnt to appreciate the existence of a great variety of substances and will have gained the power of describing their outward appearance more or less fully; and in Stage II, having learnt how to measure and weigh, will acquire the habits of determining by measurement certain properties of substances and will thus be in a position to express in exact terms the kind of differences observed; in Stage III the pupil will be led to see that profound changes take place on burning substances and that these changes involve something more than the destruction of the things burnt. The foundation is thus laid for the study of change, i.e. chemical studies proper.

STAGE IV – *The Problem Stage*

STAGE V – *The Quantitative Stage*

STAGE VI – *Studies of the physical properties of gases in comparison with those of liquids and solids. The molecular and atomic theories and their application.*

[these Stages are not reproduced]

Reprinted from the *Reports of the British Association for the Advancement of Science*, Newcastle meeting, 58 (1889), 229–50. The paper also appears in Armstrong's *Scientific Method*.

The aims and practice of teaching Chemistry
(1897)

'The development of habits is necessary for the individual, and hence for the race, but it stops development along new lines.' (Prof. G.F. Fitzgerald, F.R.S., Helmholtz Memorial Lecture, *Chem. Soc. Journ.*, 1896.)

Probably no other subject can be taught in school with greater advantage – if it be properly taught; but probably no subject is more difficult to teach properly than is chemistry. Hitherto, however, it has suffered greatly from the failure of teachers generally – especially heads of schools – to appreciate its value as an educational instrument, in consequence of their own want of familiarity with the subject as well as our failure to make its merits known; moreover, and not least, because entirely contorted views of its aims and objects have been gradually introduced, chiefly through the misdirected efforts of examining bodies, who have done irreparable injury by fostering a mechanical system – itself an outgrowth, a necessary outgrowth – of uncontrolled and narrow specialism: for if the proceedings of examining boards in general be studied, it will be found, I believe, that with the rarest exceptions they consist of individuals acting individually, meeting perhaps to consider a class-list together, but seldom seriously acting collectively on any question of educational import.

At the outset, I desire to affirm that the conventional chemistry of school primers and the various examining bodies is worthless – nay worse, positively detrimental from any sound educational point of view; and for this chemists themselves must be held to be mainly responsible.

What can be the value of a subject which it is possible

to 'get up' in the course of a few weeks or even months? That hundreds and thousands of scholars should be annually presented for examinations, and should be allowed to pass and obtain certificates after such preparation, is in itself proof of the lowness of the moral standard we are willing to accept in affairs educational – owing to the prevalence of the commercial spirit and our method of advertising 'passes' as a means of advertising schools. The discovery has, in fact, been made that examinations not only afford remunerative occupation, but also that, if carried out on a sufficiently large scale, they can be made remunerative – indeed we may class examining among the new industries discovered in modern times. Like some other modern industries – for example, the conversion of china clay into calico, the weighting of silk, the production of spirits for export to Africa – it brings considerable advantage to those concerned in carrying it out, although not always to those on whose behalf it is instituted.

However valuable examinations may be as a means of 'putting on the screw' on both teachers and taught, it is impossible to overrate the injury done under our present system by unduly 'forcing the pace' and neglecting the apparently unpromising material on behalf of those whose work is more likely to afford 'results.' The undue encouragement given to 'literary' methods, owing to the extreme difficulty of properly examining practically, is one of the greatest evils the system entails; the interference with freedom of action in schools, and the consequent check on the development of methods of training, is another; and further confusion is introduced in consequence of an entire absence of co-ordination in the requirements of the different examining bodies. It is necessary to raise all these questions, because teachers for the most part consider themselves tied hand and foot by the requirements of examiners.

To make the teaching of chemistry in schools of any value whatsoever, two things are necessary: the requirements of examiners must be such as to encourage rational teaching – indeed, to make it essential; and the character of the examinations must be such as to enforce a real standard. Instead of being allowed to nibble at a few questions and to pass if they gain the requisite minimum number of marks, students must be required to give proof of some useful knowledge of the subject, and especially of training. All who have any experience as examiners know that, tested by any such standard, the percentage of passes would not reach two figures.

When we reflect that no nation prides itself more than ours on its individualism, and probably with reason, it is most remarkable that our education should be carried out in so mechanical a manner, without reference to the necessity of cultivating and expanding what are generally recognised to be innate tendencies.

We are proud of our great public schools and talk of our victories having been won on the playing fields of Eton – yet all who seriously study the problem must recognise that our public school system is good in consequence of what is done out of school rather than in consequence of what is done in school; that the social influences which are brought to bear in them, and the discipline of the playing-fields, are the real elements of importance in the system: the school-work being of the same kind as, and in no way superior to, that done in numbers of ordinary schools of no special repute.

Why then do we not seek to apply the methods which afford such good results out of school to the studies in school? Why do we not devote more attention in school to the development of methods of forming character? Why should the whole 'civilised' world be engaged in forcing its children into one mould – in subjecting them to the tyranny of perpetual lesson-learning – in seeking to deprive them of their individuality and of the power of self-helpfulness?

It is time indeed that we paid chief attention to the discussion of methods of teaching and to the selection and training of teachers; when some advance in this direction is made, it will be possible to consider how examinations shall be conducted. At present we live in an ever vicious circle of badly examining those who have been badly taught – because both examiners and teachers have a false standard before them. Examiners' reports, when honestly given by competent men, are in consequence almost always tales of woe.

New elements of disturbance are now being introduced, as a dissatisfied public, unable to diagnose the true nature of the disease, is beginning to favour the teaching of technical subjects in schools. Examinations for scholarships are being held all over the country under the auspices of County Councils, and will – unless carefully controlled – not only interfere with the regular course of education, but have the effect of selecting scholars who may be good lesson-learners, but are not necessarily the most capable in other respects.

Before any improvement in our school system can take place, we must arrive at some clearer understanding as to the objects to be attained in schools; it must be recognised that we do not so much require to impart knowledge as to teach knowingness. We must then consider what constitutes knowingness – what are the directions in which the human mind needs cultivation in order to best fit it to perform the work of life.

And this is especially necessary at the present time when – owing to the imperfect understanding of the issues involved, of the methods available, of what might and should be done if only it were possible to really grasp the situation in which we are placed – the desire is being expressed to revert to literary methods.

Reading, writing and arithmetic – giving to these terms their broadest meaning – are universally recognised to be three necessary branches of education, but unfortunately they are almost invariably regarded as sufficient. Exception is made in the comparatively limited number of cases of those taking up careers in which the knowledge of some branch of natural science is necessary. 'Science,' in fact, is almost always taught in schools in response to outside pressure, not because it is believed that it affords an important means of training faculties which otherwise remain uncultivated. But this cannot be allowed much longer. We are, in fact, forced to recognise that if we are to fulfil human responsibilities in any satisfactory manner in the future, a fourth branch of study *must be included* in the general curriculum: it cannot be defined as science, for all exact knowledge is science, but it may be termed, for want of a shorter expression, the study of *Scientific method treated experimentally* – having direct reference to practical needs.

What we all require is to be able to utilise the opportunities we have – to be able, not merely to read, but in every way to mark, learn and inwardly digest the daily lessons of life, whatever their nature. It is essential that every possible effort be made to develop all the elements constituting character.

But so long as we merely teach children what is, and do not equip them to be – in however humble a manner – discoverers in their turn, we manifestly fail to educate them to the best advantage. Assume that it is sufficient for technical purposes to train, let us say, the bank clerk to write a good hand, to add up long rows of figures correctly, to be honest and to attend to his technical duties – yet, to properly fulfil his duties as a citizen and as a potential or actual parent, he must have received a far broader and more liberal training than will merely enable him to meet the technical requirements of his position. It is this disregard of the human side which is so fatal a flaw in the modern technical education movement; but after all it is but the swing of the pendulum to the opposite side, technical requirements having been too long overlooked in our schools.

That we must steer a middle course is only too clear to all unprejudiced students of such questions. Our present school system neither confers technical qualifications nor lays a proper foundation for the subsequent successful study of technical subjects: those who are subsequently successful, with rare exceptions, succeed in spite of, and not in consequence of, their school studies. In the future we must before all things seek to form the characters of our scholars, and to send them away from school anxious to continue their studies – not sick to death of them – and trained to work properly. The formula of modern education must be – reading, writing, arithmetic *and* scientific method, so that all human faculties may be exercised and developed.

Teachers in technical schools and colleges can do nothing with boys and girls from school so long as they are mechanically taught. My own life, I know, has been a burden to me of late years in consequence of the bitter disappointment I have year after year experienced in dealing with junior students – who, for the most part, have not had the faintest desire to learn, let alone any power of helping themselves. Brought up on spoon-food at school; incapable of thinking, because they have never been called on to think in any general manner; without the slightest power of observing; absolutely destitute of experimental skill: in all but exceptional cases they have been incapable of availing themselves of the opportunities one was only too anxious to give them and even to force upon them; and their failure has in the great majority of instances been due to faulty training, not to want of intelligence.

What is the remedy for this state of affairs? No slight alteration in our school system will suffice; there must be a radical change in method. We must recognise that the present system is a patchwork, mainly constructed of experiences gained generations ago, and we must awake to the fact that we have no longer to minister to the needs of the mere contemplative student, but to those of the practical every-day worker.

We have especially to bear in mind – as M. Berthelot, the eminent French chemist, has recently insisted – the difference between the modern era of applied science, extending over the last three-quarters of a century, and the whole development of the human race during the last 6,000 years: a difference so marked (he points out) that a new man is being created on a new earth, and the entire social organisation is being transformed amid conditions for the comprehension of which the past offers no suggestive precedents or data [*Science et Morale*, Paris, 1897].

Some preparation is required to meet this change. Mere lesson-learning must be abandoned. As Prof. Meiklejohn has said (*Proc. Int. Conf. on Education*, 1884, IV, 108), 'it is useless to force this or that idea, this or that piece of knowledge, on the minds of our pupils; all we do must be tried by the ultimate test – the test of life. That test is contained in the plain questions: Are the pursuits and the exercises followed and employed in my school likely to be carried on by my pupils after they have bid me good-bye? Will the habits I have given them remain? Are the ideas I have given them seeds that will grow and produce fruit for them in their adult life? Have I, above all, given them "the expansive joy of soul over work" that is the source of all fine art?' All must agree with him that

'It would be good work, and work enough, for a professor of education if he could show us, in each subject, how the *Didactic* (*telling* instead of *teaching*) could be kept out of the teaching of it, and how learning might be made a vigorous excursion, with fresh woods and pastures new for the dawn of every morning.'

The main object of all teaching in schools must be to train young people to be generally observant, thoughtful, exact and self-helpful – to make them desirous of extending their knowledge by applying what they already possess – to train them to pass from the known to the unknown; 'to substitute' in short, as [the Chairman of the London School Board] Lord Reay has said, 'rational for mechanical methods of teaching, in order to rouse the inquisitive tendencies which in many cases now are deadened; to make the school, not the early grave of individuality, but an attractive spot . . .'

In seeking to impart a knowledge of scientific method, it is to be remembered that children are from the outset born enquirers, and that all we have to do is to develop and practically train faculties which all possess to some extent. True Kindergarten teaching proceeds on these lines, but at school set lessons too often entirely usurp the place of exercises calculated to develop the individuality of the pupil.

Again, to quote Prof. Meiklejohn, 'the permanent and universal condition of all method is that it be *heuristic*. Man is by nature a seeking, inquiring, hunting animal; and the passion for hunting is the strongest passion in him.' When this doctrine is grasped, when this spirit actuates the work, but not before, the teaching in schools will be satisfactory.

It was necessary, before discussing the teaching of chemistry in schools, thus to consider generally the object to be attained, in order that the point of view from which the subject shall be taught and the manner in which it shall be taught may be properly taken into account. Another necessary preliminary consideration is that chemistry alone cannot be taught with advantage in schools – a general preparation must be secured by means of a course in which chemistry occupies a prominent place, but does not exclusively occupy attention.

This question is one of the very greatest importance from an educational point of view, and merits before all others the most serious attention of examining boards and scholastic legislators. To permit of subjects such as botany, chemistry and physics as alternative subjects, whilst making mechanics an obligatory subject, is probably entirely subversive of the true interests of education – such action arises from the mistaken notion that the discipline afforded by each of the subjects is equivalent, from the complete disregard of practical human requirements, and from the worship of a schoolmaster's standard of an altogether antique type. It is to be hoped that it will ere long be possible to provide a single mixed subject comprising the necessary minimum of each branch, and in which no part is treated technically.

In the case of an examination which is preliminary to others, the requirements are necessarily different from ordinary school requirements, which again may vary with circumstances – according to the class and age of the scholars and local needs; but in all cases the great object in view should be to satisfy human requirements primarily and to consider local requirements only in the second instance.

As regards the extent to which chemistry and physics should be taught, I believe that these subjects, when discussed from a proper point of view, will not give rise to any great difference of opinion – that there will not be much difficulty in agreeing as to an irreducible minimum; but in the case of mechanics and botany there will, I fear, be greater difficulty. In the case of these latter, the question of the needs of the two sexes comes into consideration: frankly, I am one of those who cannot admit that boys and girls may and should be treated alike; and in the case of girls, as the teaching of mechanics does not offer any special educational opportunities subservient to their requirements, I should not be inclined to press the subject on their attention except to a very limited extent. In the case of botany, on the other hand, the requirements in agricultural districts are totally different from those in towns: in the former it is all-important that children – boys especially – should be taught to study plants *in Nature*: to watch their growth and their different habits; but in towns the study of living plants – not of plant-forms – is all-important as affording the opportunity of studying life, and thus constituting an introduction to physiology. It is impossible for children to make experiments on the growth of animals: it is easy to make experiments on the growth of plants. To women especially a knowledge of the fundamental principles of physiology is of primary importance, and instruction in botany – and particularly in the department of vegetable physiology – is generally of more value to girls than to boys. From the point of view here advocated, botany would come late in the course, as some knowledge of chemical principles is necessary for the comprehension of vital changes.*

Obviously there is a great field for research open to teachers who will be at the pains to endeavour to devise carefully graded courses of instruction suited to the requirements of boys and girls of different ages and classes and in

---

* For a most valuable series of suggestions for such work, drafted by Prof. [H.] Marshall Ward, F.R.S., see the Major Scholarships Regulations and Examinations Syllabus, April 1895, published for the I.A.H.M.

different environments. The work done by the Committees appointed by the British Association and by the Incorporated Association of Headmasters may be referred to in illustration of what is required; but it should at once be pointed out that it will be necessary in the future, in order to aid teachers, to elaborate schemes somewhat minutely, so that those without special experience may derive assistance.

Although much experience must be gained ere it is determined what are the best modes of proceeding – for, except in principle, there can be no one mode – it can scarcely be doubted that children should from the outset be led to take note, as far as possible, of what *is* and of what *is going on* in the world about them, whilst at the same time they are being prepared for the scientific study of materials and changes.

Such preparation will involve instruction in the methods of physical measurement, and such instruction should in future form part of the instruction in elementary mathematics – a subject which, it is to be hoped, will ere long be largely taught by practical methods and with reference to ordinary daily needs.

The measurement of lengths, of areas and of volumes must be thoroughly mastered, and the measurement of mass – weighing – must be taught at the earliest possible moment, every opportunity being subsequently taken of making observations with the aid of the balance.

Reprinted from Chapter x of Frederic Spencer, ed. *Chapters on the Aims and Practice of Teaching* (Cambridge, 1897), pp. 222–59 (only pp. 222–32 are reproduced).

The Heuristic method of teaching or The art of making children discover things for themselves. A chapter in the History of English Schools
(1898)

> New times demand new measures and new men;
> The world advances, and in time outgrows
> The laws that in our fathers' days were best;
> And, doubtless, after us some purer scheme
> Will be shaped out by wiser men than we,
> Made wiser by the steady growth of truth.
>
> . . .
>
> Our time is one that calls for earnest deeds.
>
> (LOWELL)

All who seriously study the history of education in our times must agree that, although it may be long ere we can cry *Eureka! Eureka!* of an ideally perfect system, recent experience justifies the assertion that we shall hasten the advent of that desirable time if we seek to minimise the didactic and encourage heuristic teaching; for the progress made of late, which is very considerable, is unquestionably due to the introduction of heuristic methods and exercises.

But many will ask – What are heuristic methods? Even the word is strange to us! they will add.

True, it is not yet in the dictionary; but it is scarcely possible to doubt that it is come to stay, and will – nay, must – soon be there; indeed, its introduction as the watchword of a party seems really to meet a want, judging from communications I have received with reference to my paper on *Heuristic Teaching in Physical Science*, read at the International Conference on Technical Education, at the Society of Arts, in June 1897.

I first came across it in an eminently suggestive paper by Professor Meiklejohn, one of the most valuable by far of those read at the International Conference on Education held in connexion with the Health Exhibition at South Kensington in 1884.

Heuristic methods of teaching are methods which involve our placing students as far as possible in the attitude of the discoverer – methods which involve their *finding out*, instead of being merely told about things. It should not be necessary to justify such a policy in education. Unfortunately, however, our conceptions are blunted by early training, or rather by want of training. Few realise that neither is discovery limited to those who explore Dark Continents or Polar Regions, nor to those who seek to unravel the wonders of Nature; that invention is not confined to those who take out patents for new devices; but that, on the contrary, discovery and invention are divine prerogatives, in some degree granted to all, meet for daily usage, and that it is consequently of importance that we be taught the rules of the game of discovery and learn to play it skilfully. The value of mere knowledge is immensely over-rated, and its possession over-praised and over-rewarded; action, although appreciated when its effects are noted, is treated as the outcome of innate faculties, and the extent to which it can be developed by teaching scarcely considered.

Professor Meiklejohn, in the paper referred to, contends that the permanent and universal condition of all *method* in education is that it be heuristic; and goes on to say:

This view has its historic side; and it will be found that the best way, the truest method, that the individual can follow is the path of research that has been taken and followed by whole races in past times. This has, perhaps, been best put by Edmund Burke, probably the greatest constructive thinker that ever lived in this country. He says: 'I am convinced that the method of teaching which approaches most nearly to the methods of investigation is incomparably the best; since not content with serving up a few barren and lifeless truths, it leads to the stock on which they grew: it tends to set the learner himself on the track of invention, and to direct him into those paths in which the author has made his own discoveries.' It may be said, Professor Meiklejohn continues, that this statement is applicable to science and to science only. But I am prepared to show at the right time, that it is applicable to literature also, though not in the fullest extent and application of the method. The heuristic method is the *only* method to be applied in the pure sciences; it is the best method in the teaching of the applied sciences: and it is *a* method in the study of those great works of art in language by the greatest minds which go by the general name of literature. [*I.C.E.*, iv, 103.]

It would be easy to support this contention by numerous other quotations, but one will suffice – than which, how-ever, none could be more impressive or striking. I refer to the words used by Lessing: 'If the Almighty were in the one hand to offer me Truth, and in the other the Search after Truth, I would humbly but firmly choose the Search after Truth' – words already cited by the Head-master of University College, Mr Eve, in advocating scholarly teaching of modern languages. [*I.C.E.*, iv, 283].

My own career has led me along lines entirely in har-mony with the views expressed by Professor Meiklejohn – hence it is, perhaps, that I am become so strenuous an advocate of the doctrine he supports . . .

The question of attitude comes first. It is true the teaching of all subjects is now made infinitely more in-teresting than was formerly the case even in my school days, owing to great improvements in the books used, and also owing to the introduction of illustrations and demon-strations such as were formerly undreamt of; and at the same time teachers have been growing more and more consistently liberal in their views. Yet, with rare excep-tions, the attitude of teacher to pupil remains the same – it is essentially didactic; the aphorism, 'Knowledge is power', narrowly interpreted, is still the guiding principle. But this cannot any longer be permitted . . .

It must from the outset and ever be remembered that the great object in view in education is to develop the power of initiative and in all respects to form the character of the pupil. The appreciation of this contention is crucial. 'The pious Pestalozzi is filled with measureless remorse when he finds that he has *given* a little boy a conception, instead of inducing him to find it himself', remarks Professor Meiklejohn. So should every teacher be; and if the feeling expressed in this sentence can but be made to rankle in the mind of every teacher, the end is achieved. Schools will then become educating institutions; the didactic instruction which poisons our existence at the present day will be properly recognised as a fell disease.

It is necessary to insist on this over and over again, as even among those who are become advocates of heuristic training there is often incomplete recognition of the fundamental importance of observing such an attitude towards learners . . .

It is in no sense mere opinion on my part, but a conviction gradually forced upon me and established beyond all doubt by actual trial and observation during many years past, that the beginner not only may but must be put absolutely in the position of an original discoverer; and all who properly study the question practically are coming to the some opinion, I find. Young children are delighted to be so regarded; to be told that they are to act as a band of young detectives. For example, in studying the rusting of iron, they at once fall in with the idea that a crime, as it were, is committed when the valuable, strong iron is changed into useless, brittle rust, and with the greatest interest set about finding out whether it is a case of murder or of suicide, as it were – whether something outside the iron is concerned in the change, or whether it changes of its own accord.

A lady teacher who had thus presented the case to a class of young girls told me recently that she had been greatly amused and pleased to hear one of the girls, who was sitting at the balance, weighing some iron that had been allowed to rust, suddenly and excitedly cry out, '*Murder!*' This is the very attitude we desire to engender; we wish to create lively interest in the work, and to encourage it to come to expression as often and as freely as possible.

It is of no use for the teacher merely to follow an imaginary research path: the object must ever be to train children to work out problems themselves, and to acquire the utmost facility in doing so. Of course, the problems must be carefully graduated to the powers of the scholars, and they must be insensibly led; but do not let us spoil them by telling them definitely in advance what to look for and how to look for it: such action is simply criminal.

My experience teaches me also that it is the grossest libel on young scholars to say that it is useless to expect them to reason for themselves in the way necessary to follow out the simplest research; but, unfortunately, if you substitute teachers for scholars this is too often a true statement, and here the supreme difficulty of properly carrying out heuristic teaching comes in. It is the teachers who are preventing advance. Let us teachers recognise this; but do not let us overlook and misrate the powers of young children. Let us try what we can do, and if we do not at first succeed, let us try and try again; but we shall surely succeed if we can only adopt this attitude. But, if we fail, let us give up the work as soon as possible, and leave it to others to succeed where we have failed. No other policy is an honest one – for the teaching of young children should never be regarded as a perfunctory task, but as a sacred office. The whole policy of the teacher's duty is summed up in one little word, yet the most

expressive in the English language: it is to train pupils to
do. On this it is easy to base a simple test of competency.

It is needless to say, young scholars cannot be expected
to find out everything themselves; but the facts must always be so presented to them that the process by which
results are obtained is made sufficiently clear, as well as the
methods by which any conclusions based on the facts are
deduced. And before didactic teaching is entered upon to
any considerable extent, a thorough course of heuristic
training must have been gone through in order that a full
understanding of method may have been arrived at, and
the power of using it acquired; scientific habits of mind,
scientific ways of working, must become ingrained habits
from which it is impossible to escape. As a necessary
corollary, subjects must be taught in such an order that
those which can be treated heuristically shall be mainly
attended to in the first instance . . .

To this end, we must give up a large proportion of the
desk work done in schools, and instead of enforcing
silence, encourage our scholars to enter into rational conversation about the work they are doing. Why is it that
our children so seldom talk about their school work? Why
is so much trivial conversation indulged in on all hands?
Why is so much trivial literature read? Is it not because
so little encouragement is given to rational conversation
and reading at schools?

When our pupils engage together in the work of discovery and are set to find out things themselves, they will
naturally be lead to discuss their work together, to exchange views, to ask each other's advice, and they will
be so interested in their work that they will not fail to talk
about it. Nothing could be less rational – less truly preparatory for the work of life – than the system of enforced
silence we enjoin; but it is a necessary outcome of didactic

class teaching, extravagant indulgence in the use of books, and disregard of all tools and weapons other than the pen.

In all schools open in the afternoon, after the mid-day meal, I would only allow work to be done in the workshop or workroom – a room in which scholars can move about freely and do all kinds of practical work – and several mornings in the week should also be spent there. In schools such as Girls' High Schools, where the practice prevails of giving lessons only in the morning, at least two mornings should be given up to workshop exercises. It would be better in such schools to substitute attendance in the school workshop for some part of the excessive amount of home work exacted. In many schools – country schools especially – I would have little else but such work, or equivalent outdoor exercises in the experimental gardens, which will, I believe, in the future be held to be an essential feature in their equipment. Gradually I would have nearly all class rooms converted into workrooms or workshops.

The use of the words workroom and workshop is in itself not unimportant – they are good English, I believe. Laboratory – an un-Saxon term – is without significance to English ears in comparison with them; even its pronunciation gives rise to difficulty.

When class teaching is the order of the day, it is easy to exact attention and silence in the workroom by ringing a bell; at other times, teachers would constantly move about, noticing what is being done, criticising and giving brief directions to one group of pupils after another. The system is simply that pursued in many college classes. Young children will work as steadily as their elders if only they are properly disciplined from the very outset, or under almost any conditions if interested in their work. Moreover, when such a system is adopted, an effective punishment will be a few days' banishment from the workroom to the bread-and-water-solitary-confinement atmosphere of the old-fashioned class room.

Of course it will be said: 'But such a scheme is purely chimerical; it is the dream of an idealist, of a theorist who has no acquaintance with, nor conception of, practical possibilities.' Quite so! But most of my friends who were teachers in schools were good enough to say that the British Association scheme was an impossible one to carry out in practice; and yet a couple of earnest men, without preconceived views but full of commonsense, in the course of half a dozen years succeeded in applying it to a large number of scholars in public elementary schools, which, surely, are sufficiently difficult and unpromising material to deal with. Many teachers in our great public schools, I know, still hold such a view; but no one expects such schools to reform before the millennium is reached; they are in the toils of our ancient Universities, and too fully engaged in classical scholarship to consider what is good for boys generally.

After all it is mainly a question of attitude. The revolution advocated could be effected if only it were seriously entertained; if the matter were considered not from the point of view of the mere student but on the assumption that school training must be regarded as a preparation for the diversified work of life; if the heads of schools and university authorities could only be led to see that it is now necessary to substitute 'well-practised' for the expression 'well-read' in which it is usual to embody the scholastic ideal of proficiency . . .

It may be desirable that before concluding I should briefly refer to the special provision to be made in schools for experimental work; but rather by way of caution, for on this subject there has been much misunderstanding.

Architects knowing nothing of the requirements have too frequently built, and at the present time are building, school laboratories which are mere slavish copies of those provided in colleges where technical education is given; and most unfortunately, following the same example, some public authorities have declined to recognise laboratories unless provided with sinks innumerable and other elaborate fittings; consequently, not only has great expense been unnecessarily incurred, but buildings have been erected altogether unsuitable for the elementary teaching proper in schools. Instead of being put on the commonplace footing it should properly occupy, experimental work has, therefore, necessarily been regarded as a somewhat expensive luxury to introduce into a school. And this will ever continue to be the case until – no doubt in the dim future – governing bodies see that it is greatly to their advantage to consult those of us who are really capable of advising in such matters. When we are directly appealed to and asked to act as professional advisers, and architects are required but to carry into execution schemes arranged with and sanctioned by us, for which we are held primarily responsible, there will be some chance of more economical and practical provision being made. Undoubtedly we too are sure to make mistakes, and, like doctors, we shall differ considerably among ourselves, but we can scarcely fail to display some understanding of our business, and to appreciate the relative advantages of the various suggestions made, as well as judge of the suitability of the materials proposed. It is useless for architects to go about as they or their representatives often do at present, inspecting laboratory after laboratory, without ever properly grasping the meaning of what they see – consulting one teacher after another, until bewildered by the apparent diversity of opinion with which they meet, they return home in despair, and with the assistance of a clerk or draughtsman in the office – do the wrong thing for the actual purpose in view.

For work such as is contemplated in this article there must be ample room provided, but otherwise there need be no very special arrangements made.

Benches of the kitchen-table type, which need not even be fixed, suffice for nearly all purposes. These must be provided with gas, but not with water, one or two long sinks made of wood – elongated washing tubs – and conveniently situated being sufficient to meet all the requirements of a large class; more are only provocative of endless trouble and untidiness due to constant spilling of water, besides which they engender a wasteful habit of squandering water which cannot be too severely deprecated: in fact, when the day comes that we shall have taught all children at school how to wash out flasks, test tubes, etc., properly, and with the minimum expenditure of water, we shall have introduced a truly scientific procedure into our teaching, as well as into household economy. In most schools, together with movable benches such as have been referred to, it will be desirable to provide one or more benches fixed against the wall of the room, having cupboards fixed in the space underneath. Four cupboards may conveniently be constructed in two tiers under the length of bench provided for a single worker; a tray which will slide in and out may with advantage be fitted at the top of each such cupboard. It is quite unnecessary to construct the bench tops of expensive hard wood – any well seasoned wood will suffice; but whatever the wood, it should be made impervious to water, acid, etc., by ironing in paraffin wax.

As operations involving the production of unhealthy or unpleasant fumes need very rarely be conducted, a single draft closet is sufficient. This may conveniently be fixed behind a long narrow demonstration table placed on a raised platform at one end of the room.

A considerable amount of wall space behind this table should be converted into a blackboard by pinning against it by means of a light wooden framework the specially prepared black canvas which is sold for this purpose. All free wall space should have upright battens affixed to it at regular intervals, to which shelves may be attached where-ever necessary, and hooks screwed into others for hanging up things.

As to apparatus, it should be gradually provided to meet requirements as they arise, and every effort should be made to utilise ordinary articles – medicine and pickle bottles, jam pots, saucepans, etc. – and to construct apparatus in the workroom; for this latter purpose a carpenter's bench and tools, vice and files, a small lathe, an anvil, and even a small forge should whenever possible, form part of the equipment. Infinite injury is done at the present day, invaluable opportunities of imparting train-ing are lost, by providing everything ready made.

Reproduced from Education Department, *Special Reports on Educational Subjects* (London, 1898), vol. 2, pp. 389–433. Re-printed, with slight variations, in Armstrong's *Scientific Method*. The Appendices are not reproduced.

Mosely Educational Commission
(1904)

The places visited by me as a member of the Commission were New York, Baltimore, Washington, Cleveland (Ohio), Buffalo, Ithaca (Cornell University), Boston, Yale and Middletown (Conn.). But on a previous occasion, six years ago,[10] when I was three months in the country, I crossed the American continent twice from East to West, including the journey from Montreal to Vancouver by the Canadian Pacific Railway. I then spent a considerable time in the West and saw much of Chicago, as well as of Minneapolis and the great wheat region in the north-west. As a student, I was brought much into contact with Americans; this had led me always to take a special interest in them and I have all my life been a close observer of American scientific work. Any opinions that I may have formed are, therefore, something more than mere impressions derived from my recent brief visit.

It is very difficult to evaluate the part which school education plays in the United States of America. That it plays a real part cannot be doubted; but there is clearly a tendency somewhat, if not greatly, to exaggerate its relative importance as a factor in the national welfare. In point of fact, American cuteness would seem to be conditioned by environment rather than by school education. The country was settled by adventurous, high-minded men; the adventurous and restless spirits of Europe have been attracted there for generations past; the conditions have always been such as to develop enterprise and to stimulate individuality and inventiveness: so that, during the whole period in which the continent has been gradually acquired and settled on, there has been a constant invigourating struggle going on against nature in one form or another, the Indian probably having played no mean part in the education of the race. Such being the case, it is important to remember that some at least of these influences are now withdrawn and that development may, in consequence, be along different lines in future, especially as the enervating influence of machinery is also coming into play more and more.

In some respects, the Americans may be said to be a distinct if not an improved breed. Certain proclivities have undoubtedly been unconsciously selected out, and there has been much cross breeding; hence a race has been developed differing in important respects in its type of thought, if in no other way, from those represented in Europe. Moreover, success has given them belief in themselves and leads them to trust themselves. The natural resources at their disposal are boundless and their outlook is extraordinarily hopeful; they are born optimists, in fact. They have also learnt to work together and to accept and support party rule; they seem, indeed, to tolerate direction and to subordinate their individual opinions to an extent which we have difficulty in believing possible – so much so that they may be said to lack individuality. Willingness to organise and to be organised is almost characteristic of the nation. Uninfluenced by tradition, they are eminently receptive – always ready to consider and test new ideas; nevertheless, the conservatism characteristic of a young country is in many ways still manifest among them.

It is difficult to trace the development of any American peculiarities to the schools – or to find any evidence even that the schools seek to utilise and develop the national idiosyncrasies.

After seeing a number of schools in detail – both common schools and public high schools – it seems to me that

they are much as our schools; that the problems they are
seeking to solve are our problems; that their difficulties are
our difficulties. In matters of organisation and administration, we apparently can learn many things from them;
but, as regards method, it seems to me that we have very
little to learn; indeed, in depth of purpose and originality,
our best work may not unfairly be said to be considerably
in advance of theirs. But whereas here we have no general
belief in education, in America the common school system
is universally held in high esteem and its influence is very
great. The mere fact that all classes are brought together
in the common school is in itself of the utmost importance
as affecting the social outlook; even those who prefer to
send their children to private high schools seem to think it
desirable that they should first attend the common school
in order that they may consort with others. . . .

THE COMMON SCHOOLS – In interior arrangements even
the most modern schools are not superior to our own.
And there is even less attempt made in them to provide
pictorial decoration. Thring's great doctrine of *thinking in
shape* has, if possible, made less advance thus far in the
American common schools than in ours.

Much has been said of the importance attached in the
American schools to the teaching of patriotism and to the
practice of saluting the flag which prevails in them. This
involves the recitation occasionally of the formula: 'I
pledge allegiance to my flag and to the Republic for which
it stands – one nation, indivisible, with liberty and justice
for all.' This appeared to me to be a somewhat perfunctory exercise when I witnessed it. Thinking Americans
with whom I discussed the question seemed to regard the
practice as of some value in cities like New York and
Chicago, where a large alien element has constantly to be

absorbed into the population; but apparently they were of opinion that it was undesirable as a general practice.

It is almost unnecessary to say that the amount of attention paid in the common schools to reading and composition is in no way sufficient or satisfactory, the neglect of English among English-speaking people being proverbial. Apparently no greater effort is made in the American schools than in ours to lead children to read and to become really fond of reading.

The teaching of drawing is also undeveloped. Simple measurement work in association with drawing, which is being so much advocated here and which is gradually assuming importance in our schools, seems to be almost, if not quite, unknown. I did not learn that the attempt was being made anywhere to put the teaching of arithmetic on a practical commonsense basis.

Although manual training figures in the programme, the interpretation put upon the term seems to be very different from that which is usual here, drawing commonly counting as manual training. In some of the schools, where space permits, woodwork is introduced into the upper classes for boys, and cookery and needlework for girls. The belief in such work is evidently growing; but at present the schools are undoubtedly behind ours in promoting it and even more bookish than ours in their tendencies.

The Nature study lessons I witnessed, when not specifically botanical or zoological and scientific in character, were eminently superficial and worthless.

As all classes attend the common schools, these cannot be compared directly with our elementary schools, but must be thought of in connexion both with these and with all other types of preparatory schools.

There are two striking features in them – the air of refinement due to the attention paid to dress, especially by the girls, the preponderating element in most classes; and the attitude of familiarity assumed by the class towards the teacher. Distinctions, such as poverty or occupation might well condition even in a democracy, are scarcely perceptible. In America the teacher does not seem to be regarded as the natural enemy of the boy – as a person to be circumvented. The method of teaching which appears to be generally adopted involves, as it were, the constant exchange of opinion between teacher and pupil – not, as is here the case, either the communication of information to the class by the teacher or the mere wringing of what is supposed to have been learnt from the pupil by the teacher. The method has both its advantages and its disadvantages. It develops that readiness of address which characterises young Americans and leads children to give their opinions freely – far too freely many think – on all sorts of subjects; and it encourages cuteness. But it imposes a very heavy burden on the teacher and operates against close study and concentration of attention. In American schools there is no enforcement of discipline by means either of penalties or of prizes. Children are put on a footing with grown-up people and treated as young Republicans.

How, then, is discipline maintained? Is it always? Perhaps the average American boy has not such a fund of animal spirits as the English boy – he is sprung from a tolerant race and from an early age tends to ape the behaviour of his elders more than the English boy does. Certainly one great cause of good behaviour is the presence of girls along with the boys. On the occasion of my former visit, I discussed with one of the chief inspectors in Washington the reasons why the system of mixed classes had been abandoned there and then resumed. I learnt that one of the possible reasons was that it had been found difficult to keep the boys in order when alone. But undoubtedly the chief hold teachers have on their classes is consequent on their maintaining the interest of the pupils. Many of my colleagues on the Commission – not teachers – in fact, expressed the opinion on more than one occasion that the teaching was most interesting. But looking below the surface I did not feel satisfied with all that I witnessed. Whilst every teacher will admit that it is necessary to create interest, we all know that it is not always possible to maintain this at bursting point and that in school, as in the world, uninteresting work must be done sometimes; that, in point of fact, it is most important to acquire the art of doing uninteresting work in a serious and determined way. The American system seems to me to be one which imposes a fearful strain upon the teachers – especially as they are mostly women. And it has some serious consequences. One of these is inability to concentrate the attention. Everywhere the heads of the high schools complained that the pupils who came from the elementary schools could not concentrate their attention upon their work. Several were of opinion that under the somewhat more rigid conditions of the high school improvement in this respect gradually took place as the pupils moved up. On the other hand, in more than one case it was admitted candidly by the head teacher of the elementary school that the extent to which the children could concentrate their attention diminished as they grew older and passed up the school; thirty minutes, we were told, was the longest period during which boys could concentrate their attention and work effectively. This failing, I believe, is not unknown in our own schools.

PUBLIC HIGH SCHOOLS – Although we have no schools which are the precise equivalent of these, some of our higher grade elementary schools come very close to them in many respects. It is noteworthy that, in a city like New York, few who can afford to send their children to private schools make use of the public high school – one chief reason assigned being that the classes in the latter are so large that individual pupils cannot receive sufficient attention. Of those who enter, in New York, about 50 per cent (mostly boys) leave during the first year to go into business; under 10 per cent remain until the fourth year. It is said that a much larger proportion are retained in the schools in the Middle West.

In common with all my colleagues, I was favourably impressed by the way in which English literature was taught, but I could not discover that the teaching was carried to a logical end and fondness for reading inculcated. I found no more evidence that proper attention was paid to writing and English composition than in our schools; the subject which of all other is of primary importance seems to be equally neglected in both countries. I met with no proper attempt to correlate the English composition with any of the practical work.

In the teaching of mathematics and science, the American high schools seem to me to be considerably behind our best schools. I came across little evidence that the practical methods of teaching mathematics and geometry which are coming into vogue here are appreciated; and the old academic methods of teaching science seem to prevail almost exclusively. No proper foundation for such work is laid in the elementary schools.

In one respect there has been an important departure: the recognition of the value of manual training has led to the development of a special manual training department and, in some cases, of distinct Manual Training High Schools; in the latter, manual training takes the place of classics. In some cases, perhaps the majority, these are tending to develop into trade schools and to aim at proficiency in wood and metal work; they are elaborately equipped with tools. Nominally, they profess to regard the manual work from an educational standpoint, but it is quite clear that in most cases the will passes for the deed and that the teachers are not competent to develop the subjects pedagogically.

But we met with one most remarkable exception in the Brooklyn Manual Training High School. The head master of this school, Mr Larkin, has conceptions of the educational possibilities which manual training may afford which place him on a special plane. His school at present is very inadequately housed. New buildings, however, are to be provided, and it is to be hoped that these will not be so palatial and ornate as to destroy the true workshop-like character and atmosphere of the cramped quarters in which the work is now carried on. In the first year the boys do woodwork; in the second, metal work – chiefly forging; in the third, printing; in the fourth, machine-tool work. The second year work was in the hands of a man of exceptional ability, not merely a smith but an artist, so that the imagination as well as the mechanical aptitude of the boys was being well developed. The printing was in charge of a master who also taught chemistry in the school – an enthusiast who had mastered the art of printing and was teaching it *con amore*. Ocular demonstration of his persuasive powers was afforded by the presence in the workshop of a valuable linotype machine, which he had induced the makers to present to the school. We met with another man of this type teaching woodwork at a high school in Washington. He had been educated in the school and, perceiving the importance of the subject, had served for several years as a pattern-maker in the Navy Yard at Washington; then he had returned to the school as a teacher.

It is men such as these that are needed to put manual training on a proper footing – and it is all important that we should devise means of attracting such men into schools . . .

It may be hoped that Manual Training Schools – both primary and secondary – will soon be established here in which at least half the time will be spent at experimental and manual work. There is no more important experiment to be made in education than that of determining the value of such schools. In these schools a whole floor at least should be fitted up as a workshop and every kind of manual work should be carried on, so that there might be *unlimited manual temptation* in the path of the scholar, who should be free to attempt anything that he liked without following a routine course.

FEMALE TEACHERS – Most of us who are conversant with school work were struck by the distinctly low average of attainment in the American high schools. To what is this attributable? In part probably to the conditions which prevail in American life; but in large measure also, I venture to think, to the prevalence of mixed schools and the preponderance of women teachers.

Admitting that it may be possible, even desirable, to bring up the two sexes together in the earlier years of school life, I venture to think that we must sooner or later come to admit that it is wrong to do so during the later years, if the object be to develop a virile man. To put the matter in very simple terms, it seemed to me on the occasion of my former visit – and the impression was confirmed during my recent visit – that the boy in America is not being brought up to punch another boy's head or to stand having his own punched in a healthy and proper manner; that there is a strange and indefinable feminine air coming over the men; a tendency towards a common, if I may so call it, sexless tone of thought.

But if co-education be bad in itself, it becomes infinitely worse when the teachers are mostly women; they should rather be men mostly. Nowhere is the claim on behalf of women to equality with men put forward so strongly as it is in the United States. Nowhere, I believe, would it be found to be more disproved in practice, if carefully inquired into. Women have sought in recent times to prove that they can compete successfully with men in every field; they claim to have succeeded, but the claim cannot be allowed, I think. They have shown – what it was unnecessary to show – that they are indefatigable workers; and they have shown that they can pass examinations with brilliant success. But what has been the character of the examinations? Almost invariably they have been such as to require the reproduction of learning, not original effort. History records but very few cases of women with any approach to originality; it proves the sex to have been lacking in creative and imaginative power. Those who have taught women students are one and all in agreement that, although close workers and most faithful and accurate observers, yet, with the rarest exceptions, they are incapable of doing independent original work. And it must be so. Throughout the entire period of her existence women has been man's slave; and if the theory of evolution be in any way correct there is no reason to suppose, I imagine, that she will recover from the mental disabilities which this has entailed upon her within any period which we, for practical purposes, can regard as reasonable. Education can do little to modify her nature. The argument is one which women probably will not, perhaps cannot, appreciate. No better proof could be asked for, however, than is afforded by the consistent failure of women to discover special wants of their own – they have always merely asked to have what men have, to be allowed to compete with men. Domestic subjects have been taught in the most perfunctory manner possible.

Among the colleges we visited was that at Vassar – the chief college for women in the States. It accommodates

some 900 students. The college is located amidst surroundings in full harmony with the grace of the inmates: their
charm of manner overcame us completely, even in the
brief period during which we were privileged to fraternise
with them. The teachers are mostly men. The instruction
is given entirely on academic lines: lectures are delivered
on economics but I could not discover that woman's work
in the world – 'domestics' – was considered in any specific
way: it would come, I was told, under the head of technical education, which is eschewed. Apparently no use is
made of the beautiful grounds in which the buildings are
placed for Nature-study or instruction in horticulture; as
one of my companions remarked, Nature is looked at only
in the laboratory down a microscope tube.

In some of the Western co-educational colleges, arrangements have been made to provide for woman's specific
requirements, which have given great satisfaction, I am
told; but this has been done at the instance of the men
teachers.

The women teachers in America, it seems to me,
are less likely than ours are to take a feminine point of
view in instructing girls. The general environment
seems unfavourable to the development of domestic
tastes.

From the point of view that I have ventured to advocate,
women teachers must be, for most purposes, relatively
inefficient; and as teaching is an occupation in which more
than any other imaginative power, individuality, insight
and originality are wanted, it is important that men rather
than women should exercise the predominant influence.
If it be the province of education to mould the race, there
is no other question of greater importance claiming our
attention at the present time – especially as the difficulty of
obtaining male teachers is increasing day by day. In both
countries it is imperative that we should discover means

of attracting men with practical instincts and of superior mental gifts into the teaching profession. . . .

It is quite clear that the right spirit is at work in the United States; but the lack of the critical faculty and of depth of purpose, combined with an excessive development of the utilitarian spirit, are serious drawbacks at present and militate against progress in education. Until higher ideals prevail and sober calculation takes the place of a somewhat emotional and superficial consideration of its problems, it will be difficult to introduce reforms. Here our difficulty is to break through academic, conservative traditions and to arouse an interest in education: that in reality it is the most important of all subjects to be seriously considered has never yet been made clear to us either by preacher or by politician – the message awaits delivery and we need more than anything else the man to make it heard.

Reprinted from *Mosely Educational Commission Report*, London, 1904, pp. 7–25.

Sanderson of Oundle.
The fundamental problems of school policy and the cult of the turned-up trouser hem
(1924)

The late Headmaster of Oundle, F. W. Sanderson, who was brought so dramatically under notice, two years ago, by his tragic sudden death (June 22nd, 1922) on the lecture platform, at the close of an address to the National Union of Scientific Workers, will assuredly rank, in the history of education, as one of the most notable public school men of modern times, on account of his efforts to reconstruct school life, especially to imbue it with the spirit of service. Dreamer and idealist, even a mystic, in later years especially, a strange mixture of the missionary, the engineer and the scientific amateur, he gradually grew into the ethical prophet and was constructing crowns of thorns for his colleagues in the public schools, when, suddenly, and all too soon, he fell a victim to his own impetuosity and intensity of feeling – perhaps it was well, as the periods of his policy have thereby been punctuated in a manner to excite public attention . . .

During the thirty years Sanderson was Head of Oundle he raised the school from about 90 to 500 boys; he built even beyond this proportion, so that the school was ultimately better equipped than any other in the country, excepting perhaps Christ's Hospital School. Behind him was the Grocers' Company and it is meet that recognition go out to this body for the loyal and munificent support they gave to his convictions and to his labours. In time he became the complete autocrat: hence it was that he was able to put his ideas into execution with such thoroughness. No other schoolmaster, I believe, has attempted to do so much as he did and none has approached the work of school with his freedom and breadth of outlook; of course, he grew greatly in stature with time, as he gained in experience and maturity of judgment. He not only undertook but did real work in educational research – though perhaps in a rather unconscious, erratic, unmethodical way. He has to his infinite credit that he tried real experiments and not a few – a policy most teachers are afraid to face: it is not a characteristic of the clan. No other head has dared to attempt so many departures from established practice. It is as an experimentalist, therefore, that his example is most to be recommended to his profession for study. Perhaps his greatest feat was the proof he gave that the school is not the implastic mechanism it is commonly supposed to be, by showing that it was possible to dispense with the class system and that boys could be taken out of class and set to work intensively, over a considerable period, at a single subject, with advantage. I believe the tit-bit system to be the curse of our schools – it in no way resembles that of life, the child's mind being made a hopeless tangle by the multiplicity of subjects.

Finally, I must add, that only those who knew Sanderson can realise the force of his character and the persuasive charm of his manner, both the outcome of an extreme conviction and intensity of purpose.

Man's Implastic Nature

It is well known that 'though all who run may read', most prefer to walk, if not loiter, without really reading. It is for these latter, I presume, that I have been requested to make Sanderson my subject to-day and interpret his message. I do so on the understanding that he may be the thread from which I am allowed to hang a discussion of the fundamental problems of school life and policy. He definitely attempted to reconstruct the school system.

We are alike in having both been heretical warriors. Heretics do not often live to see the error of their ways and whilst Sanderson died with full belief in himself, I am an exception and belong to the disillusionised class, so can form an estimate of what is possible in this fallible but pleasant world, how few the chances of success are and the reasons of failure: how infinitely difficult and complex the task of the teacher is. I am not a mere Shavian scribe, born with a mission to spill ink for profit, though a constant kicker on paper at the shins of conventionalism. No! I am an 'old hand' of your own class – one of those poor, perverse mortals who has had the temerity to try real experiments in education and has badly burnt his fingers in the attempt.

Probably I am the complete opposite of Sanderson, having little belief in human progress, except in the mechanical arts. Also, I am in no way prone to romance but coldly critical and reflective. I would submit all things to the test of reason – whilst recognising that this is impossible. Being a 'structural' chemist, knowing how function is determined by structure, feeling, too, that our human structure is all but immutable, I have no illusions as to possibilities even 2,000 years hence. The disclosure of Tutankhamen's tomb has shown us, if it has shown us anything, that twice two thousand years ago man's sense of beauty was at least equal and probably superior to that of to-day, that his fingers were just as skilful as ours and his sense of reverence and power to wonder far higher. It must be so – the world must be eminently conservative to maintain itself. If we were not necessarily built to pattern, if any degree of variability were admissible, we should be 'all over the shop' – a crowd of the strangest abortions. The chemist has proved that we are built of shapen material, just as our houses are built of bricks, usually 9in × 4in × 3in, which can only be put together in a certain limited

number of ways. Fixity, not mutability, is the characteristic of all living beings – whether plant or animal: the
mythical story of the Creation, of each thing being made
after its own kind, is the embodiment of man's eternal
recognition of this fact. We have changed our views meanwhile and now believe in evolution, without having any
knowledge of the process and being only aware that change
takes place with extreme slowness. All that even a 'progressive' writer like Mr Wells can do is to gibe at to-day,
while picturing an exalted state, in a far distant future, of
free love in unornamented houses. Such men might learn
something of the over-mastering influence and value of
heredity and the one way of effecting improvement in type,
if they would only breed fancy pigeons or whippets or cows
yielding nourishing milk which children could drink un-
sterilised, even take service as gardeners under Messrs
Sutton[11] here – the more, if they would seriously study
anthropology, taking a dose of Dean Inge, at times, as a
corrective of their untutored enthusiasms and belief in
mental progress and the ability of man to be logical. I have
far more belief in the ennobling effect of knowledge gained
by the masses, through keeping pets and in gardening, of
the operation of the laws of heredity, than in any school
educational effort.

Our need to-day is to understand ourselves and to devise
methods not merely of overcoming our littleness but of
developing what element of greatness there is in us – to
understand something of the world in which we live, so
that we may be conscious of the severe limitations under
which we are forced to work and be of real service within
these.

Let it be clear who I am that I should dare to speak on
such a subject. At most, I can claim to have been a close
student of *scientific method* during sixty years past. I
began to teach in 1870 and can recollect the passing of the

Forster Elementary Education Act. I have taught all sorts and conditions of men and have always endeavoured to be a constructive teacher, paying attention particularly to method: dissatisfied from the beginning with the methods in use, I have sought to bring in improvements. My name is associated with the so-called *Heuristic* method, though I am in no way its author. In fact, the method is that by which man has advanced through the ages. I have merely been its most militant modern exponent and have sought, though without much success, to systematise its application. I am old enough to be long since out of fashion. I have lived, in fact, to see the attempt to develop the *experimental method* in schools a practical failure. Yet the period I overlook has been one of constant experiment and, on the whole, one of real progress – one during which much experience has been gained, if only of the restrictions which our human nature imposes upon us.

One great lesson we have learnt is, that we attempt far too much – that we fly too high in our schools: the material at our disposal, for the most part, is implastic. Let us get down to facts.

The Spirit of Service

In education we have to deal with the differences in social class, in age and in sex and with a wide range of ability, if not usually with its absence. No single system can enable us to cope with these but we can at least ask ourselves what it is we seek to do, what foundations we desire to lay and should lay in school. Surely the ultimate happiness of the greatest number should be our main object and to secure this we needs must aim at developing not only among teachers but in the community that spirit of service of which Sanderson, in his later years, was so fervent an apostle. We need to be and ever act as Christians, in fact.

Such conduct seems, however, to be impossible. The Great War, as we all know, has given rise to a greater war among us – to a mainly selfish discontent, which does not recognise the one and only means of effecting improvement – straight thinking along the lines of scientific method. Since I agreed to come here to-day, I have listened to a very powerful lay sermon delivered by Lord Leverhulme at Liverpool, bearing the remarkable title *Science, Religion and the Workshop*.[12] Strange to say, it was addressed to a technical society, the Society of Chemical Industry. It is the kind of address the Archbishop of Canterbury should be able to give to the Nation: probably the only churchman who could rise to its heights is the Bishop of Durham – who is dangerously near being outside the Church and its 39 Articles . . .

'Don't teach clerics Christianity but Mosaic morals and Christian ethics: make these the basis of your teaching', says Lord Leverhulme. Surely such advice needs no recommendation. Sanderson's message was to the same effect. Both men, too, point to 'Science' as our guide in the future. Let me add that the late Lord Avebury – the founder of our Saint Lubbock's days, the Bank Holidays – who did so much to advance popular education, was an advocate of this same view. We are told that he wanted schools 'to have a stimulating, intellectual air, charged with the oxygen of science'. Let me advise all to read the book recently published ([Ursula D. Duff,] *The Life Work of Lord Avebury* [1924]) on his work: it is full of inspiration for teachers.

Scientific Method

When Lord Leverhulme speaks of Science, I believe he has 'scientific method' in his mind – but not Sanderson's Science. It is very difficult to bring home the real meaning of the word – that which real believers attach to it. Science, in the public mind, means merely certain achievements – wireless telegraphy, to most people; the motor car and aeroplane; poison gases; the electric light; highbrow talk by Sir William Bragg and others about atoms and electrons. Almost any fool can make a wireless set work; almost every parson's son can master a motor car, if not an aeroplane. At present, the method behind all these – scientific method – is the possession of only the very few. Sanderson – who started life as a theologian – almost held it in abhorrence: he was a romanticist – carried away by the enthusiasm of his admiration of the work of scientific inquirers. Instead of reading a shilling shocker a day, as did my late friend Professor Perry, one of the greatest teachers of our time, he revelled in seeing each new scientific discovery served up to his boys as it came along. He wanted to make clear to them what science had done and was doing, to arouse their interest – he was in no way anxious to teach them the 'trick of it'. As a matter of sober fact, he had no conscious scientific method in his composition and yet he could speak of 'Real live education – boys marched up to the frontier of the unknown – to go into the world as pioneers – Darwins – Listers', forgetting that both Darwin and Lister in particular were masters of method and owed their success to methodical inquiry. Mount Everest is a recent example of the supreme value of method – in combination with Christian Ethics.

Sanderson was nothing short of inconsequent in his ravings – they were nothing less – on science. At the back of his head he had ideas which were sound in every way but he knew too little of scientific practice to be logical and was often inconsequent. To quote from the chapter on *The Ripened Oundle Idea*:[13]

The Romance of Science can be kept before boys by means of experiments and exhibits which the boys themselves arrange.

Mechanics, physics, chemistry, biology, provide a host of such exhibits and experiments. Junior boys may set up a series of historic experiments; senior boys may illustrate modern advances [p. 242].

After referring to physical measurement work and recognising its value, saying 'It must always find a place in schools', he proceeds:

It is more important at the present day to revive the demonstration methods which Huxley and Tyndall had in view. The Romance of Science we may call it; and it is romance which brings inspiration . . . The Romance of Science opens out ideals, the wondrous experiments stir up faith and belief; Physical Measurements train boys to do exact work and in doing this exact work the mind is better fitted to see and to recognise the significance of things. Both aims are necessary – to see and to do; one reacts upon the other, nor can one be effective without the other, nor can one be effective without the other. But, so far as I know, it is Romance that wants emphasising in schools at the present time [p.257].

It is to be feared that we cannot live on romance.

Probably Sanderson was spoilt by having more than an ordinary proportion of intelligence at his disposal – his school was largely filled by sons of professional men. That much of his criticism of existing school practice was sound is beyond question but he carried disregard of method too far . . .

Let me now be constructive. Scientific method is applicable to all subjects – no subject is mastered until it be reduced to scientific terms. However much we may be interested in a subject, however much we may know, we are of no use unless we can make our knowledge of service – we must learn not only to know but to do. Scientific method is primarily based upon the art of thinking effectively – therefore exactly and logically. No real training in the art of thinking is given in schools. Instead of developing the free use of mind, the natural tendency of man to follow his leader is being accentuated: children are merely taught and rarely allowed to learn.

When, recently, in New York, the Prince of Wales went out with his hat brim turned down, every New Yorker did likewise; his appearance in a blue shirt led to the hosiers' shops being forthwith ravaged for blue shirts. The tendency everywhere is to adopt the cult of the turn-up trouser hem. Some of us can remember the time when the constantly turned-up trouser was a mere aristocratic label – the sign of Eton priggishness. How the habit came in it is difficult to say. A history of the cult is long overdue. When straps went out of fashion, people for a time turned up their trousers only on a muddy day. Eton made this a distinctive ritual. Gradually, the habit was extended to all the public schools: now it is a ritual of the masses. A boy to-day may be self-determined to any extent, yet he dare not wear his trousers without the conventional tuck. The women have no such habit and are casting off tucks altogether; they are proverbially neat at the ankles and even above them, in these days. If not consciously, they have perhaps unconsciously abandoned tucks as one more sign that they will not behave as mere man does, so that evolutionists have an interesting opportunity before them – to follow man in his retrogression to the tucked and woman in her progress to the entirely tuckless state. Perhaps sub-conscious of her insecurity, woman now seems to seek that touch with nature that makes the whole world kin in always touching wood – in wearing it next her skin, discarding the fleece. Mr Wells would have all mankind think alike: one sign – it seems to be the only one that this terrible state may ultimately come about – is the turned-up trouser; it is spreading over the whole world; the only bar to universality of the habit is the unfortunate circumstance that all do not wear trousers. In point of fact, the turn-up trouser might well be made the emblem of the present state of our educational system; we shall not hail our deliverance until the Board-of-Education-Inspector dare be seen without it and concomitantly the Professor of Education ranks with the fossils: the number of tucks introduced into educational trousers is becoming alarming; so many cannot all be worn with effect.

One of them, at least, however, *must* be experimental training – training in the art of inquiry, unless man is to grow up with a tuckless mind, indifferent to all that happens around him and to the mechanism of his daily life. We have reason to believe that there is no innate tendency in man to be progressive. In his recently published Essays on *The Evolution of Man* [1924], Professor [G.] Elliott Smith does not hesitate to say that, whilst:

no one who has studied the problems of genetics is likely to deny the vast potency of heredity in determining the structure of the body and in conferring upon the individual certain generalised aptitudes of mind and temperament, the direction in which these aptitudes find specific expression is determined by the individual's personal experience and by his environment.
. . . man's mental equipment was in the past, as it is at present, derived almost entirely from the members of the community amongst which he grew up . . .
. . . The explanation of the intellectual and moral outlook of every individual and community is to be sought mainly in his or its history and not in some blind, mechanically-working force of evolution. Throughout the course of human history, man's attitude has been determined, not by the alteration of the structure of the mind but by the intellectual and moral influences which have been impressed upon each individual's mind by the community in which he lived.

If we owe our present position to scientific advance, since proverbially he who kills fat oxen should himself be fat, as many of us as possible must have some measure of understanding of scientific method. Every person of intelligence should at least know what an experiment is and have some rudimentary notion how to set about making one – as progress is and can only be through experiment.

What then is an experiment? Teachers talk of *showing* experiments, which is sheer nonsense. You can't *show* an experiment. What teachers do in their classes is to give demonstrations, in explanation and verification of statements made – an improvement on clerical method, which merely involves taking statements on faith, yet a dogmatic, not a heuristic method. The clerics, however, only appeal to miracles: teachers enact them. You will understand me when I call your attention to that delightful passage in Bernard Shaw's wonderful play, Joan of Arc, where the Archbishop – who defines himself as a sort of idol, who has to keep still and suffer fools patiently, as a teacher has – discusses miracles with La Tremouille – 'a monstrous, arrogant wineskin of a man', as is often the pupil in the teacher's eyes – a waterskin of a boy or girl. The Archbishop defines a miracle as 'an event which creates faith. That is the purpose and nature of miracles' (as of teachers' demonstrations), he says. 'They may seem very wonderful to the people who witness them and very simple to those who perform them. That does not matter: if they confirm or create faith, they are true miracles.'

An experiment as often as not has the result of undermining faith, not of confirming it – hence the Church's hatred of my class. So long as teachers merely romance and, as Sanderson advised, testify to the miraculous, there can be no progress. This is proved by the history of the Church, which is eminently romantic in its ways. Experimenting is a progressive art. In experimenting, a question is asked but not merely answered out of somebody's brainbox or by performance of a miracle – but by the methods of trial and error. It is a troublesome business. First comes a clear question, a clear issue or problem; this being stated, the possible answers are considered; one of these answers is selected for trial and a test devised and made; if the result be favourable, well and good; if not, some further reply, perhaps to a slightly different question, is sought; finally, the bearing of the answers on the question set and on the problem as a whole is considered, with a view to answering further questions. The game is without end, like the world. I have given its rules in my book on *The Teaching of Scientific Method* (Macmillan & Co.). Trumps are not always turned up: on the contrary, low cards prevail.

In learning to experiment, the student is learning to think – he is gradually developing his mind. No problem is immediately solved – a series of experiments must always be made, some to find out, others to confirm observations previously made. You may recollect Riki Tiki, the Mongoose in Kipling's *Jungle Book* story – it was his habit to run and find out: Riki Tiki's was the experimental method.

The work is not merely practical; it is largely literary. The habit is acquired of describing thoughts as they arise and things as they happen. Notes written after an event may and usually do give an entirely wrong impression – indeed, are often largely lies. The problem must be thought out and stated in writing, always before the practical work is begun; the form the initial experiment is to take and the possible answer must there and then be written down; the exact way in which the experiment is carried out and the results are next described; the bearing of the result on the question asked is then thought out and stated. The answer being, as a rule, incomplete, the best way of eliciting further information is next considered and a further experiment devised. Carried out in this way, the work has a high literary value. It is, however, slow and difficult – too slow for teachers unwilling to take trouble and impatient of results that will count in examinations. Results got by any other method, however, are rarely

otherwise than worthless as training. The real reason of
failure is that the teacher, as a rule, has never learnt to be a
detective – apparently the detective is born, not made; the
drill sergeant is more easily constructed out of human
material, which likes to boss; moreover, to do what one is
told is far, far easier than to think out a course for one's
self. I always recall the pathetic appeal made by a young
thing in a teachers' class at one of the training colleges:
'Please, teacher, won't you dictate something?' The
teacher had been urging her to think. In fact, the method
is one by which it is sought to overcome a prime short-
coming of our human nature; I will not call it a fault,
because if we all took to thinking for ourselves the results
might be awkward. Still, it is the method by which
Science is built up and advances – *the* method of science.
I will only say, as the result of fifty years' experience, that
I believe it to be far more widely applicable than has been
supposed – given enough good-will to apply it. At present
it is not in general use, even in the Universities. Here I
must correct Sanderson. I cannot forgive his saying:

> The science master must not be misled by the many fetishes with
> which it is sought to adorn educational theories. Such fetishes
> are often the prelude to deathly reaction. They appear in many
> guises – character, culture, 'educating to think'. All these may
> lead the schoolmaster away from his one purpose. The main
> purpose of education, as we conceive it, is none of these things;
> its purpose is to get more of life, of creativeness [p. 239].

Creativeness is a fine word but just what does it mean?
Another quotation:

> I believe we want to get away from formal 'training to think'.
> Boys come to school to do something and not to learn. Learning
> will come as a by-product [p. 248].

No one believes more in 'doing' than I do – but the
'damned boy' needs drilling. We forget this and ever
twaddle of playing upon his interests, because of the introduction of the feminine spirit and emotionalism into

education to-day. Experimenting means constantly doing but doing always with a clearly thought-out purpose, the eyes being used in every direction – unfeminine habits.

The Hyde in the man, not the Jekyll, was speaking when he thus advised. That a man of his intelligence and liberal outlook could utter such an opinion is a matter of no slight significance, however, as showing the difficulty we have in making clear the method of science.

Still, Sanderson's bark was ever worse than his bite and he was always an inconsequent creature, for he could also say:

It is not sufficient to say that science should be taught in schools. The time has gone by for this. *We claim that scientific thought should be the inspiring spirit in the school life* [my italics]. Science is essentially creative and co-operative, its onlook is onwards towards change, it means searching for the truth, it demands research and experiment and does not rest on authority. Under this new spirit all history, literature, art and even languages, should be re-written.

He here grants all that I would ask for – the same man is speaking.

Though he could thus bark at culture, he was himself a man of high culture and, besides preaching 'service and science', advisedly trained his boys to use books. In my teaching days, the boys who came to us from his school were distinguished by their ability to get up a case in the library – few from other schools had had this training.

Trained as a mathematician, he early took to engineering and was the first to establish an 'engineering side' in a public school (Dulwich). At Oundle, he gave special attention to workshop work but it is open to question whether his method was a good one, sufficiently systematic. Still, in schools where too much is always attempted, it is difficult to carry out ideas.

Lastly, he was one of the very few who have sought to make school 'punishment fit the crime': he never pro-

claimed a boy a fool because he did badly at this or that
subject but took pains to find out what he could do
with advantage. In this particular he showed a Christian
spirit which is usually lacking, especially in most classical
masters.

The great advance in schools, in my time, has been in
buildings, in the introduction of improved surroundings,
not in the methods of teaching. Read Hugh Miller's
account of his school days – a book every teacher should
know by heart – and you will realise how good was the
early Scotch system – it was thorough, not too much was
attempted; it was individual, the scholar did the work
[*My Schools and Schoolmasters* (1854)]. To-day, examinations and Board of Education Inspectors are the dominant partners: the cult of the turned-up trouser hem prevails everywhere, together with an un-Christian spirit of
competition and dominance – the very contrary of the
spirit Sanderson and Lord Leverhulme have advocated.
Control is in the wrong hands, in literary hands, in the
hands of men of words. Sanderson was right in claiming that the school was the place for doing, not mere learning.

We are clearly at a fateful period of our history and must
be up and doing if we are to save ourselves and worthily
administer our empire. We need to understand the arts of
ordinary life – the benefits of right doing and the evils of
wrong doing, especially in food. In its complexity, our
task is one of terrible difficulty. We are not only ruining
our race by over-breeding at the wrong end but we are
failing to produce leaders in sufficient numbers; our country is grossly over-populated and for the most part can
only live on coal – which we will not use with effect.

An address delivered at the Sixth Annual Conference of the
Reading and District Teachers' Association, 26 September
1924. Reprinted from *Education*, November 1924.

Notes to Introduction

1. This was printed by his son Edward Frankland Armstrong, *C.*, 35 (1938), 3. Biographical details have been drawn from this and *Eyre*. After Huxley's death his house 'Hodeslea' was bought by Armstrong's brother-in-law, the tobacconist and lepidopterist, Robert Adkin.

2. The 'chaos' of contemporary scientific subjects compared with classics is documented in W.A. Campbell and N.N. Greenwood, 'How we got our Sixth Form Chemistry', *Chemistry in Britain*, 5 (1969), 62–6. Note also D. Thompson, 'Science Teaching in Schools During the Second Half of the Nineteenth Century', *S.S.R.*, 37 (1956), 298–305.

3. W.H. Brock, 'Prologue to Heurism', in *The Changing Curriculum*, History of Education Society, 1971.

4. Based on lectures given at the London Institution in 1869 and published in 1877. Armstrong detested the book as 'rank and pretentious' and an 'injury to rational methods', *S.M.*, 408.

5. J.P. Phillips, 'Liebig and Kolbe, Critical Editors', *Chymia*, 11 (1966), 89–97; Sir Harold Hartley, *Studies in the History of Chemistry*, 1970, 195–222; C.A. Russell, *The History of Valency*, Leicester, 1971, *passim*.

6. R.C. Trench, *On the Study of Words*, 22nd ed. revised by Rev. A.L. Mayhew, 1892, viii. On Trench see *D.N.B.* and M. Trench, *Letters and Memorials of R.C. Trench*, 2 vols., 1888.

7. *C.*, 35 (1938), 11; Armstrong incorrectly dated the case as 1879, and was followed by *Eyre*, 64.

8. Compare C. Bernard, *An Introduction to the Study of Experimental Medicine* (1865), Dover reprint, chap. 1.

9. E.C. Robins, *Technical School and College Buildings*, 1887; Robins's letters to Armstrong *I.C.A.*

10. Armstrong never understood engineers. He confronted

student engineers with heurism when they were 'least receptive of aught else but the practical side of engineering', and failing to interest them, he developed a bias against the engineering mentality. See *J.S.C.I.*, 60 (1941), 85, and *C.*, (1934), 1–14.

11. *Eyre*, 73–4, 86, 286. See J.C. Evans, *A New Course of Experimental Chemistry*, 1892.

12. *E.T.*, 37 (1884), 287–8. Armstrong's paper was not printed here, but in *I.C.E.*, iv, 97–120. There was no discussion of Meiklejohn's paper.

13. *I.C.E.*, iv, 103; *E.T.*, 37 (1884), 288; partly quoted by Armstrong below, 106. Compare J.M.D. Meiklejohn, *Inaugural Address Chair of Education University of St Andrew's*, Edinburgh, Glasgow and London, 1876, 34.

14. *Inaugural Lecture*, 30: 'How shall we best introduce heuristic methods and set young minds upon the track of scientific truth?'

15. 'Heuristic Instruction in Physical Science', *International Congress on Technical Education*, 1897, 8–13. In this he defined the heuristic method as 'the absolute antithesis of the didactic method' (10), but did not imply that it was the first time he had used the word. *Eyre*, 112, suggests that the term was first used by Armstrong at the British Association meeting at Newcastle in 1889, but this is not supported by the printed *Reports*. According to O.T. Onions, ed., *Oxford Dictionary of English Etymology*, Oxford, 1966, 439, the word 'heuristic', meaning 'serving to find out', was derived from the Greek *heuriskein*. The word 'heurism' appears in the *Introduction, Supplement and Bibliography* to the *O.E.D.* (Oxford, 1933), but not in *O.E.D.*, vol. 5 (Oxford, 1901).

16. For a polemical account of Rousseau's influence, see G. Bantock, 'Discovery Methods', *Black Paper Two*, 1969, 110–18; on the Edgeworths and heurism, see *S.S.R.* 50 (1968), 423–32.

17. Gladstone, a pupil of Liebig, was a physical chemist of private means. Like Armstrong he believed that Great Britain had to develop a school curriculum which 'would fit the young for the practical work of life', *I.C.E.*, ii, 82. He was a member of the London School Board from 1873 to 1894, where he advocated spelling reform, object lessons,

manual training, and the teaching of elementary science. See *D.N.B.*; W. Tilden, *J. Chemical Society*, 1905, 591–7; and *B.A.R.*, 1903, 429–30.

18. *B.A.R.*, 1887, lxxviii. According to *Browne*, 4, Armstrong's campaign was supported by a Committee of the Chemical Society. Neither printed nor manuscript sources at the Society support this.

19. A.M. Worthington, *An Elementary Course of Practical Physics*, Edinburgh, 1881; *idem*, *A First Course of Physical Laboratory Practice*, 1886. Worthington (1852–1916), who had studied with Wilson at Rugby, deliberately selected experiments of a quantitative kind. He found that pupils were capable of getting results 'quite sufficiently accurate to suggest or confirm the correctness of the principle involved without taxing too much the practice or the intelligence of the young experimenter', *First Course*, 2. Since his courses were not constructed to train specialists, but to evoke 'in the boys a genuine and generous interest in natural phenomena, and of training them to habits of patient and conscientious study' (*ibid.*, 4), their Wilsonian pedigree is readily recognised, and their appeal to Armstrong understandable.

20. W.H. Brock, *Atomic Debates*, Leicester, 1967, study 1.

21. *S.M.*, 362. Compare Worthington, *First Course*, 6–7. Needless to say, such expedients were influential and are still much used in British undergraduate laboratory teaching.

22. Worthington's Clifton course had cost £70 for laboratory fittings, £40 for apparatus, and an annual running expense of £12.50 (*First Course*, 9). Armstrong discussed laboratory fittings in detail in *S.M.*, 452–71.

23. *Eyre*, 113. On Stuart see Armstrong, *J. Chemical Society*, 1933, 469–71 and *N.*, 1 (1933), 194–5.

24. *B.A.R.*, 1903, 420–9. For Ward, see *N.*, 42 (1890), 620–6, and below, 108, and letter L.C. Miall to Armstrong 23 January 1896, *I.C.A.*

25. Webb to Armstrong 20 March 1899, *I.C.A.* Armstrong's designs (note 22) influenced Felix Clay whose *Modern School Building* appeared in 1902; see 2nd ed., 1904, chap. 5. Also T.H. Russell, 'Some Practical Notes on the Planning of Science Laboratories' in F. Hodson, ed., *Broad Lines in Science Teaching* (1909), 2nd ed., 1911, 252–67.

26. The children performed experiments publicly in 1900, *S.M.*, 393–9, and 434–44. Armstrong loved showmanship. One of the more exciting children's Christmas entertainments in London in 1926 was a playlet at the Royal Society of Arts entitled 'Alice in Wonderland at the Breakfast Table', in which players and audience together investigated the properties of carbon. *N.*, 117 (1926), 166.

27. An emphemeral picture book by Hugh Drummond. From 1899, the children's activities were based upon an allegorical story, 'The Three Water Giants', published in W.T. Stead's periodical *Books for the Bairns*.

28. *Browne*, 14–16; *Eyre*, 135–6 and 275–80. Four of the original six books are in *I.C.A.* Eyre felt that had they been published they would have become reference works 'illustrating what can be done willingly [and] enthusiastically by judiciously prompting and guiding the young inquiring mind' (136).

29. Browne (1865–1961) retired in 1926 to become a Science Tutor at the London Day Training College, where he influenced several teachers in the 1930s. See *S.S.R.*, 43 (1961–2), 187, and E.H. Rodd in *Browne* (1968).

30. G. Van Praagh, *Chemistry by Discovery*, 1949; E.H. Coulson, 'Nuffield Advanced Science–Chemistry. An Account of a Stewardship', *S.S.R.*, 52 (1970), 261–71. Van Praagh, a pupil of Browne's who taught at Christ's Hospital from 1933 to 1964, became a Nuffield Research Fellow in Chemical Education in 1964.

31. *Essays on the Art and Principles of Chemistry*, 1927, xix–xx. Kipping's remark is also revealing: 'H.E.A. and the Chemical Society were practically the same thing; officially he was the Secretary, but in fact he was the Director, and when he was elected President his rule was supreme', *C.*, 35 (1938), 59.

32. *S.S.R.*, 2 (1920), 197–212. See C.L. Bryant's 'Fifty Years On', *ibid.*, 32 (1950–1), 140–5. The phrase 'science for all' was probably first used by Vassall to describe his course at Harrow. See *B.A.R.*, 1917, 149.

33. A symposium on heurism published in the same year as Westaway's book showed that its spirit was not entirely crushed (*S.S.R.* 11 (1929), 65–70).

34. See the debate in *Nature*, 145 (1940), 863, 1023; 146 (1940), 133; also L. Connell, 'Demonstrations and Individual Practical Work in Science Teaching: A Review of Opinions', *S.S.R.*, 52 (1971), 692–701, and compare Professor Kerr's conclusion that the British emphasis on individual practical work had made it 'inflexible, repetitive, outmoded, and often inadequately integrated with theory', J.F. Kerr, *Practical Work in School Science*, Leicester, 1963.

35. J. Bradley, 'Bread or Stones of Nuffield Chemistry' in *Black Paper Three*, 1970, 87–90; *Education in Chemistry*, 4 (1967) 58–64. Bradley's interesting heuristic scheme was published in nine parts: *S.S.R.*, 44 (1963), 549; 45 (1964), 365; 46 (1964), 126; 47 (1965–6), 65, 72; 48 (1966–7), 467; 49 (1967–8), 142, 454; 50 (1968–9), 87. In the Nuffield science schemes traditional syllabuses are curtailed to allow more time for different methods to be used. In Stage I of the Ordinary Level chemistry syllabus, 'Exploring Materials' a modified heuristic approach is used; but in Stage II, the ideas and theories of chemists are described.

Notes to Texts

1. *Perry*. John Perry (1850–1920), Irish Professor of Mechanics and Applied Mathematics at Finsbury Technical College.

2. *Micraster*. A genus of the fossil shell *Spatangidae* (sea urchin) which abounds in chalk; named after its star-like arrangement.

3. *Rowe*. Arthur W. Rowe, a Margate doctor. In his forties, encouraged by family seaside holidays at Margate, Armstrong became a distinguished amateur geologist. With Rowe he mapped and photographed the coastline of the British Isles. See A. W. Rowe, *Proc. Geological Society*, 1900–8, *passim*.

4. *Lancastrian Frankland Society*. See H. E. Armstrong, 'First Frankland Memorial Oration of the Lancastrian Frankland Society', *J.S.C.I.*, 53 (1934), 459–66.

5. *Graphic or Glyptic formulae*. Structural formulae introduced by A. Crum Brown in 1864 and adopted and adapted (largely for pedagogic reasons) by Frankland in his *Lecture Notes for Chemical Students*, 1866. See C. A. Russell, *A History of Valency*, Leicester, 1971, pp. 100–7.

6. *Hofmann* A. W. Hofmann (1818–92), first Director of the R.C.C. He left London for Berlin in 1865. See Armstrong's brilliant study of Hofmann, *J. Chemical Society*, 69 (1896), 637–732.

7. *1851 Commissioners*. In 1894, through the efforts of Lockyer, Mundella, Huxley, and Playfair, Imperial Research Fellowships were created from moneys provided by the Royal Commission for the Great Exhibition.

8. *Sprengel tube*. Apparatus for density determinations; the U-tube pyknometer devised by Hermann Sprengel.

9. *Fletcher oven*. A simple cupboard furnace heated by a Fletcher, or ring, gas burner, and used in quantitative analysis.

10. *six years ago*. Armstrong's visit to America and Canada in the summer of 1897 was made under the auspices of the Association of American Agricultural Colleges. See *Eyre*, pp. 126–8.

11. *Sutton*. 'Sutton's Seeds' – the large horticultural merchants in Reading where Armstrong delivered the paper.

12. *Lord Leverhulme*. Leverhulme's Second Messel Memorial Lecture (Armstrong gave the first), on 'Science, Religion and the Workshop', was published in *J.S.C.I.*, 43 (1924), 242–50.

13. *Ripened Oundle Idea*. Armstrong's quotations were drawn from [H. G. Wells, ed.], *Sanderson of Oundle*, 1923, chap. 6.

Bibliography

Many of Armstrong's educational essays were collected in his *The Teaching of Scientific Method*, 1903 (2nd ed., 1910, reprinted 1925). His letters and offprints are housed in Imperial College Archives, London, for which see *Henry Edward Armstrong, F.R.S., List of Correspondence and Papers*, offset Imperial College, 1967. The definitive biography of Armstrong is J.V. Eyre, *Henry Edward Armstrong*, 1958; unfortunately its division into three sections and the absence of an index make it difficult to use. C.E. Browne, *Henry Edward Armstrong*, privately printed for the Chas.E. Browne Book Fund by Harrison & Sons, London/Hayes/High Wycombe, 1954, is a charming account of the work at Christ's Hospital. This is reprinted, together with a memoir of Browne by Ernest H. Rodd, in *Henry Edward Armstrong and Charles E. Browne*, 1968. The heuristic experience is also described in L.F. Morris, *A History of St Dunstan's College*, priv. print. for the College, London, 1970. Two other interesting and critical reminiscences are E.G. Walker, 'Finsbury Technical College' in *Central*, 30 (1933), 35–48, and H.E. Armstrong, 'The Beginnings of Finsbury and the Central', *ibid.*, 31 (1934), 1–14. Sir Harold Hartley's essay on Armstrong in his *Studies in the History of Chemistry*, Oxford, 1971, places Armstrong in the context of the history of chemistry. The apparent revival of heuristic methods in the 1960s is discussed by P.E. Richmond and A.R. Quraisha, *School Science Review*, 45 (1964), 511–20. The standard sources on the scientific movement in nineteenth-century education are: D.M. Turner, *The History of Science Teaching in England*, 1927; J.W. Adamson, *English Education 1789–1902*, Cambridge, 1930; D.S.L. Cardwell, *The Organisation of Science in England*, 1957 (2nd ed., 1972); C. Bibby, *T.H. Huxley, Scientist, Humanist and Educator*, 1959; M. Argles, *South Kensington to Robbins*, 1968; R. J. W. Selleck, *The New Education 1870–1914*, 1968.

Index